# Hey You... Relax!

## 100 Smiles, Laughs and Whispers

Sharon Ramkhelawan

ISBN: 0692407375
ISBN-13: 9780692407370

# ACKNOWLEDGMENTS

Praise Jesus for mercy, for Hope….
new every single day.

Thank you to the Hope Press Team (Ruth Archibald,
Leslie 'Jodi' Brown, Fanny Nandulaal, Tiffany Simon,
and Michelle Solomon)

# CONTENTS

# PREFACE

A treasure chest you may not find
Within the pages of my mind
Convictions you may not hold dear
Perhaps some contradictions here...
But truth I pray will be its fame
And for these ramblings I'll take blame
So when my life endeavor's spent
I'll know I've offered my 2 cents.

So these are the ramblings of my unpredictable mind.
Hope you're inspired or in any way affected.
Blessings,
*Sharo*

# THE FRIEND, THE STENCH AND THE SPARROW

A friend of mine said, "If you don't start writing again, our friendship is over." For the past several weeks my life has been a whirlwind of meetings, events, launches, openings, construction, upheaval and every other verb that springs to mind. While there remains no viable excuse other than laziness to account for my reluctance to wake up at 5am and whip my sleepy mush of brain cells into coherent thoughts, I feel like few things in life are as valuable as a great friendship. So here I am.

Outside, the New York morning is eerily quiet. Even at 5 on a regular morning, you can hear the sweet sounds of sirens and warbles of cab horns punctuating the air and puncturing your ear drums. My living room windows are open to let in the cool breeze and let in the morning scents of... of... what is that smell?

I hear birds. I really do. While the Gotham-ish city struggles to arouse itself, the birds are chirping merrily, and I hear them from my 10th storey window. Apparently, they don't have to ride the subway this morning, and they must have missed the 5 o'clock news about the swine flu pandemic and surely they would not be chirping if they knew about the economic state of the country?

We are bombarded on every side by things that take our chirp away. But the sparrows know something that we sometimes forget: "Are not five sparrows sold for two pennies? Yet not one of them is forgotten by God. Indeed, the very hairs of your head are all numbered. Don't be afraid; you are worth more than many sparrows." Luke 12:6-7 (NIV)

Father God cares about the sparrows...
Why should I feel discouraged?
Why should the shadows come?
Why should my heart feel lonely
And long for heaven and home?
When Jesus is my portion
My constant friend is He
His eye is on the sparrow
...And I know He watches me.

So chirp, chirp and chirp AGAIN for this is the day that the Lord has made and I WILL rejoice and be glad in it!

He watches over you today, working all things out for your good. Even though I know my friend shamelessly used our friendship as a weapon to get

2

me to write again... there aren't many friends who care
or appreciate me so much... so "thank you!"

# THE ROCK

My trip home on the subway is usually my time to unwind my tangled thoughts and muscles, let go of the hassles of my wearying employ and look forward to a few hours of rest. Yesterday that didn't happen.

I squeezed my body into a jam packed subway car and to my horror there were more people squeezing in behind me! The apologetic look on my face was meant for the person in front of me - whose space I was about to involuntarily invade. Luckily, the doors shut and we were on our way.

Then, like a runaway jet on autopilot, my mind raced around the day's events, the To Do lists, the things I can't change but would, the things I can change but wouldn't, the people I miss, the rainy evening... and before I knew it, my heart was overwhelmed.

I bowed my head and stifled a cough that was

threatening, the kind of cough that comes up when you're about to cry and the cough let me down. Trust me, the last thing you want to do on a sardine-packed train when there is a threat of swine-flu, is cough. I couldn't help it... I coughed. It was almost comical how the space around me cleared up a couple centimeters!

It was then I felt Holy Spirit's presence, sandwiched in that crowded car with me. "When my heart is overwhelmed, lead me to the rock that is higher than I." And I thought, "That is exactly where I want to be... led straight by the hand, up into the presence of the one who knows my name." He lets me mount up on wings like eagles and lets me soar over the storm and crowded subways. At that Rock, I sit in His shadow, protected against the strong winds that blow and the blistering heat of day. When the door opened at my stop, I emerged with a quiet confidence and a calm assurance that:

I have a Father
He calls me His own
He'll never leave me
No matter where I go

He knows my name
He knows my every thought,
He sees each tear that falls
And He hears me when I call.

The next day I headed back to that subway, but without the overwhelmed heart. Trust me, the reason why you go to the Rock with an overwhelmed heart, is to give it to Him… wholly and completely.

# IS THAT MY CELL PHONE VIBRATING
# OR MY STOMACH GRUMBLING?

Whether we choose to accept or deny it, the truth remains that the world has changed by leaps and bounds in the last decade or two and keeps changing more every day. If you're younger, a decade seems like a really long time - if you're not, you use terms like, "it's ONLY ten years."

It would hardly surprise me if one day, on National Geographic, they're exploring a rural jungle tribe of humanity, running around in loin cloths and bamboo piercings and suddenly, the short native extracts his cell phone from his strap of clothing. Really it wouldn't. I know people who still don't have running water or a flushing toilet, but have a cell phone. What a world!

Anyway, gone are the days when you had to wait two weeks for a reply to a letter you mailed overseas. Now you can be instantly upset or worried when someone doesn't answer an e-mail.

As wisdom increases, the very things devised in the minds of men to simplify life, are sometimes the very ones that complicate them. The same pill that melts away fat is the one that causes heart murmurs and high blood pressure. The same 100K car that shines like a black diamond is the one that becomes a death trap with an inebriate behind the wheel.

Sure, technology has all been moving along, since the wheel was invented or as they say, some caveman made fire.... but it's undeniable that the increase of knowledge has been exponential in the past 50 years.

One thing's for sure though... knowledge and wisdom are two completely different things. Knowledge invents the car... wisdom tells you not to let anyone drive it who has been drinking.

The word of God tells us that these are the days of increased knowledge and it also records in Psalms that, "The fear of the Lord is the beginning of wisdom. Those that keep His commandments have understanding."

Today take a moment to recognize the truth of God's word, appreciate its relevance and poignancy and know that not one word of it will pass away. Did you hear about the guy, Ben Southall who just got the job to live in a fantastic house on an island in Australia and do incredibly arduous tasks like bar-b-que, snorkel and blog for $100,000 a year? The news reports that they had applications from every country in the world except North Korea and a couple African nations. That's probably only because the guy in the loin cloth didn't get cable yet.

# HEY YOU... RELAX!

If I could put time in a bottle... I would shake the heck out of it and ask it why it takes so long to go by between 4pm and 6pm when I'm at work and wanting to go home time speeds by laughing while I'm spending time with people I love, or at the church and generally not at work.

Before all the realists, psychologists and physicists explain to me that it's not the actual passing of the increments of time that speeds up but my enjoyment of that time space makes it's passing seem faster; I'd like to say that at 5:30am I'm already wishing it was 5:30pm.

No, I'm not this way every day and neither are you. What I would like today is to attack the day with all my might and live it to the fullest, stuffing each millisecond with meaning and purpose. Instead, I am wishing I had a few spare hours today to better prepare my lesson for tonight. Thank God for His

Holy Spirit that gives me the strength, energy and the words to speak when those times come or else all you'd be hearing from the pulpit would be "z z z z ".

But wonderfully incredible IS the life that pours into me when I speak His word, sing His praise and I am among His people. All fatigue drains and I feel rested and rejuvenated. You know when you sit at a desk for 10 hours and you feel like the energy has been sucked out of you? You exerted no real physical energy, you sustained minimal movement or impact and you certainly burned little to no fat or calories, but yet there is that exhaustion? Well therein lies the dichotomy of life in His Spirit.

Even if you sat still in His presence, the fatigue washes away. At the very least, even if you remain tired, the stress falls away like abandoned backpacks of lead and there is peace. If you don't believe this then you've obviously never experienced it. (That's an invitation.)

So, today as you read, I pray for you, yes you, my stressed out friend, to relax! May your happy minutes, though fleeting, be overwhelming and abundant as you rest in the knowledge that our God, your Abba, is not subject to time! He operates and exists outside its constraints and boundaries and can bless you, meet you and certainly watches over you this moment.

See? There's that peace again. Now if He could just show me how to pull off a Star Trek-ish transportation and totally skip the subway to work, that would be fantastic! "Beam me up Scotty!"

# MY CASHEW TREE

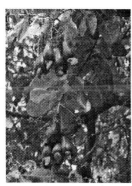 The cashew tree outside my Godmother's house was a 9 foot paradise for me. With branches in all the right places for my little feet to climb, I would spend countless hours perched on the highest branch of my hot air balloon, concord SS jet, Mt. Kilimanjaro, Tibet and the Great Wall of China. There was no one else with me except maybe the cute missionary pilot or the bald monk in the saffron colored robe. That was more than 3 decades ago.

A few Christmases ago I went back to that house and the little cashew tree was still there, with small orange fruit and cashew "nuts" attached. It didn't look like a grand mountain, a wonder of the world, a technological marvel or an exotic country... it just looked like a little cashew tree. Where had all those dreams gone? In my childish eyes, that tree was my vision of a great and marvelous world. In my adult eyes, it was sadly, far less.

Maybe that's part of what God meant when He said, that "unless we become like little children then we cannot inherit the Kingdom of God." Unless we can look at something small and not just imagine but enjoy, anticipate and become immersed in the grandeur of what it can be... then we have not begun to have that childlike faith. When we're like children, we see our circumstances today and KNOW in our hearts that something SO MUCH GREATER is on the way. We understand that the world, the earth and all its beauty was made by Almighty God. It's ours to see, to enjoy, to reach with His love... because He so loved, HE gave His life.

Once more, I will climb up on my cashew tree of faith, and with childlike vision allow God to take me to places I have never seen, heights I've never ascended and journeys I have not yet taken.

# WAITING FOR RAIN

On the 14th day of a 21 day fast, in the middle of the night I felt so parched, dry and stretched out like arid ground. Like my spiritual "tongue" was covered in sand, cleaving to the roof of my mouth. I needed the water of life. I was so desperate and more than anything, I wanted to end my fast. So on the 14th night, I decided that I would pray about it. I asked God to please let me know if it would be OK to break my fast 7 days early and I earnestly hoped He would say "Yes."

I woke up the next morning weeping at the amazing glory of our God. During the night I had a dream from God, unlike any other I've ever had in my life. I saw images that would be burned on my memory forever and even now as I write I am amazed by the clarity with which I can recall them. Up until that time I had never had such a prophetic, admonishing or directive dream as this and I am still amazed and humbled that the great God of heaven would speak to me in such a marvelous way. Fifteen years or so after this dream, I still see God unfolding aspects of it and bringing it to my memory.

My directions were clear. I went on to fast 7 more days and every time the pangs of hunger and the need for food came to me, those images from my dream rushed to my mind and the hunger vanished. I fasted with joy and expectation, hope and awe... I had not experienced that before - in that measure- during a fast.

Fasting helps refocus our attention on the One who is most worthy of it. There is a thirst in the soul that many are convinced can be filled with substance, emotions and even people, all of which are passing away. It is the deepest part of our spirit which responds to the Holy Spirit. The only way to describe the result of that connection is "satisfaction".

Before that night, I was dry and He rushed over me, filling up and saturating my thirsty soul. Every dry dessert became new and whole again. There's no doubt that the water is always so much better when you've spent a long time... waiting for rain.

# SHARO'S WALK OF SHAME

Some time ago, my husband Curtis, put me out of the car. OK... maybe that's not exactly what happened, but it's close. He stopped by the intersection and I got out because I thought surely, he wouldn't drive off and leave me standing there in the middle of the cold, dark night. Well, I thought wrong.

After the shock wore off, I started my "walk of shame" to my house and after 2 steps I saw the error of my ways. I was upset for something that didn't even make sense (no it wasn't PMS), and when he refused to be part of the problem I was creating, I decided to prove a point by getting out of the car. LOL... Now it's funny to me... funny and stupid.

I walked past the houses on my street and some people were sitting outside, watching me funny, some said "hello". I smiled back. I noticed that there were actually stars in the sky, I picked out Orion. I tried to formulate the apology I was going to present to my husband... but I felt like he wouldn't... no, SHOULDN'T accept it. I walked slowly.

As my house came into view, I realized that I forgot the whole apology. I walked up to the door and almost ran into Curt. He was going to come looking for me because I was taking too long. Well I apologized... profusely. He accepted kindly and now I'm staying put in the car.

It's just like when we don't understand God you know. He requires some things of us that seem too difficult or we just get upset because He's taking too long to answer us, so we do something stupid. We separate ourselves from Him. We stop praying, reading the word, attending church... and we wander alone. Are WE trying to teach God a lesson? Make a point? Foolishness. What point can the pot make to the potter?

Sometimes it's in those times alone that we realize how lonely, dangerous and sad life can be when we're separated from God. But you know, if we look through the darkness we see that His eyes are always on us... waiting for us to come home.

Then He smiles because we've made it safely and learned a valuable lesson.
I DID.

# DAVID CROWDER LOOKS WEIRD

Thanks to one of my friends, I saw David
Crowder in person. I sat only 3 feet away from where
he was singing. A girl next to me, maybe 13 years old
or so, after staring at him with her jaw hanging open
for what seemed like an hour said, "He looks weird!"

I turned my gaze to David and thought, "Hmmm.
He could certainly be filed under 'weird'... easily."
From his Arabian-esque/Caucasian beard to his
everywhere curly hair and his skinny, extra-tall body
to his teeny specs... he was quite a sight. Then he
opened his mouth and praise started rushing past his
lips. "There is no one like you; there has never, ever
been anyone like you!" Hundreds and hundreds of
people, including me were jumping and dancing and
singing every word right along. It seemed like
everyone knew every word to every song. That weird
guy really gets around! God's into weird... when
weird's for His glory!

Remember weirdo Noah? Building a huge boat, in the middle of the nomadic dry land, for over a century, waiting for "rain"? Yeah... well everyone thought he was 100% certifiable, but Genesis 6:8 says "But Noah was different. God liked what He saw in Noah."(The Message)

What about that other one - John? Living in the wilderness, wild man, eating honey-dipped-bugs (yummo)... his beard was wilder than Crowder's. Here's what God said in Luke 7:28, "I tell you, among those born of women there is no one greater than John." (NIV)

So Mr. Crowder... you're in excellent company! Come to think of it... my family  is entirely weird, not to mention my good friends (weirdoes every one)... and I'm pretty weird too (see pic reference). So go ahead... celebrate the weirdness that makes you a remarkable servant of the Most High God and use it for His glory!

Webster's definition: Weird - *of strange or extraordinary character; may imply an unearthly or supernatural strangeness or it may stress queerness or oddness; mysteriously strange or fantastic.*

# POKE THE DEAD LEG

You know that deadness that crawls up your legs when you've sat in the same position for a long time? As long as you sit still... it's OK. You could poke at your leg and not even feel it, your foot hangs lifeless and you can't get it in your shoe because you've cut off your blood circulation by sitting on it. Hmmm... that happened to me.

We drove 5 and 1/2 hours from Weatherford to Houston without stopping... and my left leg "fell asleep". When I recognized that numbness, I tried to stay motionless, because I remembered the pain. I remembered how uncomfortable it feels when that blood, all of a sudden, rushes back into those veins... OUCH!

As a little girl I would try to stomp on my brothers' feet at that time... they couldn't run away if their feet were numb. LOL

We do that in our God-walk too: staying in the

same position, sitting on our behinds and refusing to get up and do His will, and our spiritual legs go numb. As long as we stay in limbo, unmoving, there is no pain. So many of us chose to stay that way. Lifeless, numb, unaffected, riding along... it's easier.

To "come to life" would cause us too much discomfort. But that's what the Holy Spirit does. He rushes through our veins when we decide to pick up our cross and follow. At first it hurts. It's uncomfortable and you think, "Maybe I should have just sat there." But soon, the life comes flowing back into you. You're alive! The pain is gone! The numbness is gone! You can walk! You're free to run, dance, jump and be fully alive in Him.

So go ahead, poke that dead leg, shake it up, grit your teeth and know... that in HIM we live, and move and exist... Fully alive!

# POTATO-CRUSTED-FISH-FILLET

It seemed like every time I turned the TV on... there it was. Captain "someone" had a new fish fillet that was covered in what looked like hash brown crust... on TV... over and over ... there it was. It may not sound yummy to you, but while I was fasting... I felt like I would have given 3/5 of my spleen to taste it.

So after the fast the first thing I bought at the grocery was the Captain "somebody" potato covered fish fillets. I put it in my buggy along with all the other "healthy" treats I picked out and tried to ignore the "you'd never eat that" voice in my head. I paid for it, took it home, put it in the freezer. It's still there. Unopened, in the box. That was more than three weeks ago.

And you know what else? I haven't seen the commercial on TV since then! Hmmmm... go figure. When I was hungry for food and meditating on those fillets, it seemed like I could see them everywhere. Now that I'm no longer desperate for it - I can't.

It's no wonder that, when I'm hungry for God's will, meditating on Him, I see Him everywhere. I look around and EVERYWHERE I see people who need to know Him and His love.  But when I'm not desperate for Him... it seems like I can't find a sign, a sinner, a soul that I can reach.

I want to know Him more than I wanted those fillets. FAR FAR MORE. That's the prayer of my heart. To keep that utter desperation for Him so like David I search for Him with abandon. Look for Me and you will find Me, He says. I say, "I will".

# HERE COMES THE SUN- NATASHA RICHARDSON

The first time I saw the remake of the movie The *Parent Trap*, one scene embedded itself in my mind. It's in that part of my memory where I store things that make me smile. Lindsey Lohan, then just a child, runs her finger along the sparkling, hanging tear drop crystals of her mother's lamp. The crystals catch a ray of sunlight, and the music of chimes starts in the background to begin the melody of "Here comes the Sun". To me, it was breathtakingly simple and yet profound.

When Natasha Richardson's character entered the movie, the sunshine did too. I remember thinking, "Oh I love her, that's who I'd like to be." Even though it was not her most renowned or prolific performance, it was the one that I treasure best. When she looks at her frightened daughter and in her beautiful accent says, "Not to worry darling, not to worry," I smile every time.

When I saw the news of Natasha's passing, I was sad for her family, especially her boys. Suddenly, I heard the song in my head again and I thought, I wish someone could tell them, "Not to worry darlings" and I wish it could be her. In Christ, there is always the truth that the "Sun" is on His way. Malachi said, "But for you who fear my name, the Sun of Righteousness will rise with healing in his wings. And you will go free, leaping with joy like calves let out to pasture." (Malachi 4:2) (NLT)

Today if you find yourself in sorrow, I pray for comfort in grief, and hope in loss and somewhere, somehow, a ray of sunshine. I pray for you my friend. That the God of all grace, comfort, strengthen and protect you, gives His angels charge over you and guides you throughout what will be for you, a wonderful day.

# A LESSON FROM A 2 YEAR OLD

They teach you that you don't start an article, blog, etc. ... with a conversation that happened in a car, but that's exactly where this one begins.

On the way home from church I was minding my own business, sitting in the front passenger seat, unwinding. It had been a long day. We had church, dance practice and I helped move pieces of sheet rock, lumber and other garbage from a demolished wall. I was tired but content to be on my way home.

Then it hit me... a view that took my breath away. It was a huge mass of grey cloud with the suns rays beaming by the hundreds from behind it. The rays sprayed all across the city of New York in the distance and a brilliant silver lining edged the massive grey cloud. This would NOT be the point at which I cliché myself into the proverbial corner but it was the moment I held my breath and remembered why I am where I am. I remembered my little nephew Jesh, who was on my mind for much of yesterday, singing,

"You paint the morning sky,
With miracles in mind.
My hope will always stand
For you hold me in your hand
Lord I'm amazed by you."

When he was two, he lay on a bed, weak and very ill. He had been having a dangerously high fever and seizures and was in the middle of having one when my brother put his hand on the baby's head and did the best and only thing he could. He prayed. My brother laid the sick child on the bed as he shivered with fever.

Jesh, at two years old had not yet started to speak. His communications were an amusing combination of gibberish and clicks punctuated by the occasional word like "drum". Jesh could not speak but even at the age of two he had an amazing and prodigious ability to play the drums. Today the doctors had said that there was nothing they could do to stop the seizures, we had to hope for the best. This is where Yeshua (Jeshua's namesake) steps in. At that moment laying on the bed, Jesh who couldn't even speak, began to sing in his sweet little voice:

"You dance over me,
While I am unaware
You sing all around
And I never hear the sound.
Lord I'm amazed by you."

He drifted off to sleep and later when he awoke, was completely healed.

He's been perfectly healthy ever since. That's where my mind went when I saw the clouds and that's where my mind is this morning.

 Update: Jesh is nine now. He not only plays and has won numerous contests for drum playing, but he masterfully plays the guitar, bass and piano as well. In fact, at age nine, he just finished his first audio CD, in which he played every instrument and sung every part of a three part harmony.

Till today, if he ever gets the sniffles, the flu or any sickness he already knows the solution "Prayer". He prays for others. Today I remind you of the scripture that says "He rejoices over you with singing." When was the last time anyone rejoiced over you? Your Father does. Today my heart says one thing, "Lord, I'm truly amazed by you."

# TEARING DOWN THE WALL

Building construction is not my forte but when it's my project, I'll get my hands dirty! By God's amazing intervention, today we signed the lease on the first official meeting place for HopeNYC church... there was a problem though. There was a wall. A wall smack dab in the center of what was supposed to be the sanctuary. You know it had to go.

On Sunday afternoon as I conducted dance practice I had to pause to look as Curtis demolish that wall. Something about seeing it come down was fascinating to me. Granted it was no Berlin, but still a sight. Also interesting was what was left in the aftermath: a wide open space and a pile of rubble.

I feel an analogy coming on and the Pastor in me has to mention that sometimes when we tear down the things in our lives that hampers our growth, (toxic relationships, bad habits and even a job that has you so stressed you're sick) there is a freedom that comes at the breaking point. A wide open space of liberation is in your sight and it feels good. At your feet, though, inevitably lies a pile of rubble.

That ugly pile is reminders and remainders. They are traces of those things that you gave up that keep popping up to suck you back down into destructive behavior.

So, on Sunday, I stopped the dance class, and piece by piece, we moved all the pieces of that old wall to the garbage. It took work, sweat and bruised fingers, but in the end, the wall was gone. That's what it takes for a new start. It takes you dealing with remnants of your struggles and moving them away. It takes blood, sweat and tears to clean up the mess. But before you start dreading the process, I've got some fantastic news. Your redeemer, shed the blood, poured the sweat and cried the tears for you already. He's removed every piece of the mess and rubble, carried it on His shoulders, to Calvary. There He left it. You are free.

Now, where that wall stood, there's a clean open space. One day soon, people will fill that space to worship the God of heaven and I will be there (and if I get what I want... so will you!).

# MY LIFE BUDGETING…

This morning I'm sitting quietly in my chair but scurrying hurriedly in my mind. Ever done that? It's not fun. It's like when Curt goes to the ice-skating rink. He's usually hanging on for dear life to the rink's walled edge with his legs and feet way ahead of the rest of him. That's where my mind is... way ahead of the rest of my body this morning.

Strange enough though, this morning I'm thinking about what Henry David Thoreau had once said, "The price of anything is the amount of life you exchange for it."

As I contemplate getting "all dressed up" to join the mad masses at work today, I think about the price I'm paying. How much life am I exchanging and how much value is being added in that exchange? Tough question... Almost triggers my upchuck reflex.

My thought today is that whatever I do, I will try

to ensure that when I exchange a part of my life for it, it's close to a fair trade.

That's why I will take the time to talk to my Maker, read His word, and love my family, my friends and those around me. To exchange my life in these ways is to make an investment and exchange life for things of worth.

Today I will believe firmly and steadfastly in WHOM I believe, the God who has never failed to be a personal part of my life and I will not be bullied into the status quo. At the end of this day, I will have less life left to exchange... therefore I will spend it wisely.

The best way I can start is by telling you who read this that you are special to me, and I pray that God grant you peace, love and His Holy presence all through this day!

# READ TO LIVE...

"Wake up, wake up", I can still hear my mom's voice and feel her fingers tickling under my feet. That's how she woke me up for school. The gentle insistence was followed by my arms and feet flailing about, me pulling the sheets over my head and cocooning my body in a stubborn refusal.

She wouldn't stay. She always retreated to the kitchen and I was left there to decide. Choose between drifting back into the comfort of sleep and risk being late for school or forcing myself out of inertia to brave the cold shower of my "no hot water" home.

I still marvel that I chose to get up and postpone the instant gratification, every time. I'm not sure what it was that made me study extra after homework without being asked, or do crazier things like "read for fun" but one thing is without question, my mother incited me to learning. She still reads voraciously and so do I.

Even today, the only thing that makes me look forward to taking the subway home is the book I happen to be reading. Mark Twain once said, "The man who doesn't read good books has no advantage over the man who can't read them."

I still get slightly suspicious of the "smart" people who can't answer the question, "What are you reading right now?" Don't think you don't like to read. You obviously understand its power to connect, reveal, incite and influence. You're reading this book.

In 39 years of living, nothing I've read can come close to comparing to the book I still read every day. I've read the Bible from front to back many times, and will again. Each morning, it gives me incentive to throw off the covers and face the day... at least there are no more cold showers!

Why not start right? As motivated as you may feel in this moment, my prayer is that you are spurred to find the treasure of the word of GOD. He is Life. He is Truth. He is the Way. It's a smart thing to "know the way, before you go." May this day be a fantastic one for you my friend!

# NEED A HAND?

Here's a secret... I would love to say something deep and stirring, but it's too early and I'm way too sleepy to form any semblance of cognitive motivation in my mind. It's not that the words, thoughts and emotions are not there... they are, but on some mornings I can't find them. I think about all the things I have to get done at work today and I think my brain groans and sputters.

My mind feels like one of those times when I know what I want to wear, that purple shirt, and I look through every drawer and closet and can't find it. It's in there... I just can't put my finger on it. Granted, later when I'm NOT looking for that shirt... there it is!

Strikes me as important though, to realize that we traverse this earth for a few years and this day is as important as any. Chances are I will encounter people today who are as depressed or happy, or conceited or humble, or kind or self-centered as they were the last time I met them... but this remains true: You cannot pull someone up, unless you're on higher ground.

Thing is though... it's hard to climb when much more welcoming than the view from the mountaintop is the view at the back of my eyelids and the sound of a low, contented snore. (I don't snore... I think.)

So this morning, I'm stretching my hand upward, like the little girl reaching up for her daddy, because from there, the view is so much better. I may not have the climb in me... but He's already there! That's who God is to me today. The one who makes a tomorrow brighter and gives me a much better vantage point than the one I get on my own two feet.

I don't know how things look around you right now, but "Father God's eyes roam about the earth, looking for someone to show Himself strong on their behalf." I hear myself: "Here I am Lord!" Maybe now would be a good time for you to do that too! Now I have to try to figure out where that purple shirt is.

# GET OUT OF JAIL FREE?

I WOULD LIKE TO SHARE A TRUE STORY...

The Police left two messages on my work machine, 2 on my cell phone and 2 on my home phone. They sent emails to my work, home and church addresses (scary the information they can find! I just moved here!)

"Sharon Ramkhelawan from HopeNYC please call concerning the April 12th Easter Egg Hunt." That's it. A foreboding swept over me as I heard the message, but I called immediately. The female on the other line, was direct and taking promptings from a male officer whose voice I could hear in the background.

"Ask if she has a permit for this?"
"She needs to come in and let me see it. I can't believe they issued that."
"She cannot have an event of this size in this area."

"There is no parking."
"There can be a riot when you give away anything."
"We cannot allow it."

I went to the precinct to meet him. Even while we spoke I prayed, "God please intervene. Spirit of God just work on his heart and mind, and grant me your favor Lord. Let every curse be a blessing..."

And once more, God showed up. I eventually heard all about the officer's daughter coming in from college and his brother-in-law who is also a minister. We talked for a long time about family, history, geography, society, computers and almost every other topic under the sun. I even got a "clergy card!" Not quite a "get out of jail free" card but a really official card that says I am a friend of the police force and a member of the clergy... the first one I ever had... even after all these years of ministry. I was excited!

I'm going back for more talking the next free moment I get. He's a very interesting person, full of stories and histories. So, the egg hunt is on... WITH security! Praise be to God, He always answers prayer and has a great way of working things out for your good!

Update: When I first wrote this piece (*6 years ago*) I had applied for my first public event permit in New York. Since then, God had opened doors where the police come out in dozens to our events, including our first Christmas parade in 2014. For the first time in Queens history, the entire stretch of Rockaway

Blvd from 101st to 145th was shut down for a church to celebrate Christmas. God continues to amaze us.

# A GOOD MORNING...

Today I feel good. People who live with me might say, "Why?" You should be frazzled, stressed or disappointed but certainly not good. I'll tell you why I feel good... because yesterday God held my hand.

Sure, He is the Omnipresent God, always there, but yesterday He showed up for me. No claps of thunder and blinding lightning, no shaking of the mountains and pillars of smoke, just a still small voice in my solitude saying, "I order your steps, and nothing, SHALL BY ANY MEANS, harm you."

Last night I sat in awe of the Elohim and wondered about the day He revealed Himself to Moses and the Israelites. I am still in awe. So many religious sects and persuasions are based on one person getting a revelation from a higher being... but the camp of Israel, all the people heard His voice from the mountains, saw His presence... and shook. As amazing as that is, all the revelations of Himself to

Israel cannot take the place in my heart of who He is to me. As I read in the book of Exodus I remember why those words are so important to me... because they are a revelation of who He is. Every word, read properly, reveals His holiness, His justice and most of all His love.

One day that Word became flesh and lived among us and we looked at the glory of God, in Adoni, the Messiah. He still comforts the weary... Binds up the broken... Frees the captives... And I am in awe.

This morning my heart is glad to have received the knowledge of Jesus Christ. Very glad! If you know Him, then you understand. If you have not yet received that kind of information, I'd be more than happy to tell you EVERYTHING I know!

# NO MORE CUCUMBERS IN SPICY MARINADE!

Several sautéed mushrooms
1 avocado wedge with chopped Pico and spicy vinaigrette
1 whole fried plantain
1 large Potato wedge
1 Fried Chicken drumstick
Macaroni and tuna salad
Cucumbers in a spicy marinade

No it's not the recipe for heartburn, it's what I had for lunch yesterday. I went to a small eatery close to where I work and walked circumspectly around the isles of culinary choices and picked out a little of everything I had an inkling for. By the time I was done selecting, my clear container was full with a hodge podge of edibles and I was hungry.

Pity we can't be that selective with everything in

life! "Lord I'll take 2 scoops of sunshine today, no rain with that. I'll take a little bit of a raise, 4 more hours of sleep, a public holiday, a day at the beach, a few birthday presents and a tiny vacation to Maui... hold off on the cheese."

There's a commercial on TV that says, "Life comes at you fast..." how true, but it certainly beats the alternative! (It not coming at you at all!) Here comes the cheese: Life's a buffet of experiences, good and bad, sweet and sour, and it's not those experiences themselves but the choices we make with them that shape us into the people we are. The choices are seldom simple ones... but always there to be made.

Even though I cannot blame Holy Spirit for encouraging me towards that cucumber concoction, listening to Him in real times of doubt and indecision leads me to the right choices. And you know what... if (and when) I make a mistake that's ok too... I can choose to not take that path again. It was Einstein that said, "Anyone who has never made a mistake has never tried anything new." I don't think I'll be having those cucumbers again! I ate everything else. The container was empty and I was full!

# A GUAVA, A PIT BULL AND A TINY KERNEL

Late yesterday I stood on the platform waiting for the unsurprisingly late train to arrive. I was tired but I was glad. I had a big, ripe guava in my bag that a friend gave me which I intended to consume as soon as the train arrived... and the end of Thursday evenings always bring a special cheer to me because the work week is coming to a close.

There were maybe 5 or 10 people waiting around me at the same spot on the platform, all haggard and exhausted looking. One guy was scaring me because he looked like he was verging on epileptic seizures. I removed one ear bud and to my relief I heard the definitive sounds of rap music blaring out of his headset. OK ... so at least the fits were not medically related. Was I tired? Sure... Was my job frustrating? You bet your sweet bippy! Was the brackish scent of urine wafting from the concrete floors making me a little queasy? Most certainly... but I still couldn't wipe the smile off my face.

The smile was because though the world around was brimming with reasons to be bogged down, forlorn and at least stoic, between my ears, I was absorbing buckets full of Living Water!

See, I hit the inspiration jackpot! I wasn't listening to "Must have been love, but it's over now" and I certainly wasn't rocking to "one night stand music", No. I was listening to someone telling me that the word Caleb means "dog" and even though the world may have seen that as an insult, Caleb had the fortitude and tenacity of a pit bull. He bit in to the promises of God and didn't let go till they came to pass. By the time the train arrived, I was almost hopping with excitement and didn't even realize that I was an hour late. But I was right on time for a timely truth spoken right into my Spirit. Sometimes, even in the midst of a whirlwind, God gets through to the ones He loves.

When the world's bearing down on you and pressures of living are wearing you down, bury yourself, immerse your soul, and become totally absorbed in the truth of His word. It will always amaze you how His word peels away the husks around your cob of happiness and when the doors open, you emerge refreshed, revived and renewed. May this kernel of a story bring some of God's truth to your heart, and I pray that this day, you are fully blessed!

# LOOKING FOR HOME AGAIN

The other day we went house hunting. With no real location in mind we drove around looking for realty signs and properties that looked like a place we'd not mind living. My thoughts immediately raced back to a time in Texas, when Curt and I were again, looking for a place to call home. Our budget was tight, as it is now and everything we looked at was either very trashy, in a bad neighborhood or way too expensive. That was a while ago and the house I left in Texas felt like home.

The day before I bought that house though, out of sheer fatigue and frustration, we had almost said yes to a fixer upper. I think calling that house a "fixer upper" was a gross exaggeration of the actual state. It was bad. My heart was heavy, I didn't feel it was right, but I didn't see any options.

That, my friend, is Jehovah's signal to step in. When the children of Israel stood at the raging shores of the sea with a thundering army following fast behind them, they were out of options. When they stood before the threatening Goliath, I'm certain no option seemed a viable one. 10 years ago when I stood in the face of an enemy who said you have 2 weeks to get out of this country, it seemed I had no option.

In stepped God. His strength is made perfect in our weakness. It's when our arms fall to our sides and our exhausted wills surrender; when we truthfully say, "There's just no way..." He makes one. The skeptics may say that sounds like the fabrication of a romantic mind. I say, "You believe whatever suits you, that's an option He gave you, and I will believe in Christ!"

So like the parting waters of that sea, and the shepherd with a sling that slew a giant, and the check for a full year's salary that God provided that very day I was threatened, and a million more instances in my life and yours, God WILL make a way. Whatever your situation, if you abandoned it to His mighty hands, then at this minute He's working it out for your good!

Updated: Did GOD EVER step in. That day I saw houses I liked but could never in my wildest dreams afford. But I imagined and knew that somehow GOD's plans were big. I found an apartment that I loved and we lived there for a little over a year. Then one day, miraculously, God sent a servant with the finances for a house for me. The house I now live in is one I had seen on this particular day, from the outside, and thought, "could it ever be?" All I can say is this:

Now all glory to God, who is able, through his mighty power at work within us, to accomplish infinitely more than we might ask or think.

# HOP ON ONE LEG AND SAY "WUBBA WUBBA!"

If you went to Miss Ivy's private school as a child, you were fortunate to be treated to Sesame Street every morning at 10am and again in the afternoon at 3pm. This was when Cookie Monster was just that, a cookie lover and proud of it and not some nutritionally and politically correct, trite "veggie monster." Mr. Hooper (or was it Cooper) still ran the store and the last thing on any one's mind was the sexual orientation of Ernie and Bert. Those were simpler times.

Now, problems are way more complicated than wishing that the moon was a cookie, you know: 65 hour work weeks, rents and mortgages, crumbling economies, terrorists and a morally deteriorating, evermore depressed populous, among other things.

It makes no sense to pretend that our problems don't exist, to act like that pain in our back isn't really there or to look for someone to place blame on. I believe a more commendable and rewarding choice would be to decide "what am I going to do about it." See, having faith that the problem will go away is nice but getting up and moving in the direction of that faith is obedience... faith without works is dead... being alone.

I think sometimes we become stuck in a Sesame Street solution. Case in point: Prairie Dawn's computer is not working, she is distraught, when... lo and behold... it's a bird, it's a plane... It's Super Grover to the rescue! He proceeds to exercise his creative license and solve Prairie's issue all at the same time. His solution to her problem? Jump up and down on one leg and say "wubba wubba". Needless to say, it is an exercise in futility but it certainly was funny.

Sometimes in the middle of your situation, or when someone you love is in need, you feel like all you're doing is the wubba wubba... you are making no dents in the debt and no improvements in their health, that broken heart is no closer to wholeness and for all your noblest efforts, that mind is still not at rest. But you have something Prairie didn't. No... not a blue monster with unusually large eyes. You have an Abba Father who has given you a treasure in earthen vessels! You: the earthen vessel. The treasure: His light in you that shines in darkness. That power of God is in you, so that all will know that it is HIS light which brings hope in an otherwise dreary world, to the Glory of God the Father.

Today, you are that light. So shine on! He who began a good work in you is Faithful and will complete what He started!

# FIRST CLASS BUBBLES

Upgrades are overrated... sometimes. I remember paying $700 odd dollars for a ticket to Romania and then being curious about how much it would cost to fly first class. The answer? $4,000 big ones. It's true. I'm not making it up. 3 grand more for a bigger seat, a longer menu, free booze, complimentary $1 headsets and a flight attendant that gives a hoot about your well being. That's the cost of an upgrade.

So, as of this moment, I will continue to squeeze into the less than ample coach seat, eat the chicken enchilada dinner and sip multiple glasses of seltzer (they don't give you too much in those little glasses).

Yesterday I flew back to New York from Houston and slept most of the way. Do you know how difficult it is to look dignified when you're asleep on an airplane? You've seen those people: Head tilted back or ungraciously to the side, mouth ajar and breathing sounds coming out. I think if you fly first class your mouth stays closed (it should for what it costs). Either way it was not an unpleasant flight and I must admit I was tempted to pay the extra $200 to upgrade to first class. I didn't.

I think about how different it is at HopeNYC. I can't speak for all the other places in the world, but I must admit, I feel pretty special every time I walk through those doors. Not because I'm the Pastor there (even though that is a true honor and pleasure for me), but because in that space, I am so very aware of who I am: A daughter and servant of The Most High. First class. That's who we are in EVERY SPACE: children of the Almighty because the earth is the Lord's and the fullness thereof.

Your Abba Father is the King of Kings. That is an honor and you, my friend, are the apple of His eye. Once I fell asleep on the train, for a few minutes, and jerked myself awake when I popped a nonexistent bubble I dreamt I was chasing. Yes. Everyone saw and everyone laughed but that's another story. Too bad there's no upgrade on the Metro...

# MEET THE PARKERS

With each new day comes a new challenge. As certain as taxes are the situations that make your prayer sound like toddlers who just heard the sound of the ice cream truck, "Oh please, please, please, please, pretty please!" It's 9:17pm and I've been driving around in my little car since 7:45pm looking for a parking spot. In my mind I've already come up with 7 or 8 excellent inventions to oust other cars from their cozy positions and insert my tiny red vehicle. Know what's ironic? For now, I live in PARKchester and I can't ever find a place to PARK!

Thanks to a trickle of foresight, I have my trusty MAC and apparently quite a chunk of time on my hands. Hence, this story is written from a parking lot.

My friend just called.

Her: "Sharo, what are you doing?"

Me: "Sitting in the parking lot. Been driving around for more than an hour"

Her: "Oh…you didn't find a place yet?"

Me: "Um…no, that's why I'm still sitting in my car"

Some more conversation… then I say, "Pray with me so I find a spot to park." I expected her to say, "OK. I will."

Instead she says, "Lord, give Sharo a spot to park now please."

"Sharo, a spot will open up right in front of your apartment!"

"I know! I agree!", I say and rev my engine and put the gear in drive with my foot on the brake. Ready. See, surer than taxes is the truth of God's word that says, "If two people would agree on anything in His name He will do it." Add a dash of faith and voila. There is one small challenge. One other guy is in front of me in this line of waiters. Wait a holy second…is he leaving? There he goes! He has given up waiting and now I'm first. Wait another second batman…. there's a man walking across the parking lot…key in hand. A smile breaks across my face. Could it be?

He is walking, walking, straight up to the parking spot in front of my apartment. He gets in his extra large SUV and starts backing out! Praise be to God. Before that behemoth of a vehicle even backs all the way out, here am I in my red ladybug of a Chevy, pulling in. I have 2 feet in front and behind my car in my awesome parking space! Praise God. It is time to do the Happy Dance of parking! Have a problem? Call a friend to agree with you in prayer.

# ALONE IN MY BED

 Curt has been in Trinidad for a while so I've been sleeping alone. It's an introduction not a confession. Without Curt things are different to put it mildly. My bed is big and empty and I'm sleeping without earplugs.

He's not aware of this, but even though he often falls asleep on his side of the bed, by early morning he's usually in the middle. Since he is a bit heavier than I am, he sinks the middle down so I am perched on a hump or I roll down into the middle too.

Now that he's not there, I fall asleep on my side of the bed and wake up on my side of the bed. Last night I thought, "This is a big bed, I am going to use it all". I

scooted to the center puffed up my pillow, and went to sleep. I woke up this morning, on my side, bordering the edge. Whole big bed... me in a corner.

Sometimes we fall into habits without realizing that we are. Life forces us to limit our hopes and expectations. We are almost afraid to believe that God can do whatever we think or ask... we are afraid of being let down. So we remain hoping for small changes, "Just a little bit Lord" is all we are whining for.

We forget that He's the God that makes a cruise not run out of oil until every pot in the entire town is full of oil. He's the God who took 5 loaves and 2 fish and fed thousands. Same God.

No... It's not easy to believe when things are getting tough. But He NEVER fails. Hope in Him is never futile. Even though you may not understand your circumstance, take comfort that He does... every moment. So move to the center, stretch out your legs, spread your arms open, uncurl that body and relax. This is your day.

I'm excited for Curt to come home but I think I'm going to try sleeping in the center again tonight. By the time I get the hang of it he'll be back.

# FINGER ON THE HORN

Today I'm sitting at my desk, in my own office, writing this story and I'm so elated I could cry. In the other room my fabulous administrative assistant, Michelle, is piddling around... doing something constructive. So what if she can't make coffee? She sings like a nightingale.

God is amazing to me and while the enlightened world that doesn't believe He exists, struggles with unanswerable questions that have no foreseeable resolve; I put all my unanswerable into His omniscient care... whew!

My assistant is still trying to put the coffee on and just told me the coffee machine is making "really weird farting noises." *chuckle*

The past six to eight months in New York have been a whirlwind. A whirlwind of events punctuated with the consistent flying debris of the lack of parking spots.   One thing is for sure though, amidst the swirling of events and circumstance, is the undeniable stability of the knowledge of God's presence.

I've learnt to move with the pace of a larger city and the crowds of the subways. I've developed a blind eye mentality and non-working nose sensibility  to many of the metro's sights and smells... and I drive with my finger on the horn.

I now understand that it's not so much offensive as it is informational: to honk your horn in New York.  How else would the guy in front of you know that the light has turned green? How else would that pedestrian on the cell phone with the baby on her hip, who stops in the middle of the street to tie the laces on her converse, know that you're coming around the corner? How else would you get the taxi driver that comes to a dead halt in the center of the street, to hurry up? Ok, so maybe I still can't honk as liberally as most New Yorkers do, but today I discovered that I'm driving with my finger on the horn.

All in all, I stand amazed at the master plan of my Master God. He sees the first and the last and makes all things beautiful in His time. He takes all our yesterdays, mistakes included and fashions a fantastic tomorrow... an end and an expectation.

My assistant just informed me that the coffee is

"falling" and that is a good sign. Here's a cup to a fantastic day for you my friend, all in the design of your Abba.

# WHAT'S A LION GOT TO DO WITH A SLUG?

It's happened again. Just when all the pieces seemed to be falling into place, we were starting to have a smooth routine and my schedule seemed handle-able, everything erupted again. There was I, rolling merrily along when my Abba turned that light on in my head and said, "Do this".

"Oh Lord", I argued, "Curt is not going to like this."
"But He'll expect it" He replied.

So here we are again in the middle of a

"renovation". HopeNYC's building looks like it vomited it's insides on itself. Bare walls, dust and paint, pieces of wood and screws all around… and no room to store anything

valuable.

It's like a sleeping lion to me. When it awakes, it slivers open its eyes at first, scoping the periphery and adjusting to the light. Then it stretches out its paws and legs and rolls its neck around. And then, as if to let the entire world know that the lion has awakened, it ROARS.

While the work is being done, it's difficult to discern the impact but when it's ready, oh what a roar. Just like you... and me. People may not be able to discern the impact of what God is molding you into... but when He's finished... Oh what a roar!

I try to live so His work can be done in me. I pray that the artist that He is, would break me, melt me and mold me into whatever He designs. All the while the creation process may be uncomfortable but, His word ALWAYS accomplishes what He set out to do.

So don't sweat too much when life gets uncomfortable... your Father's blueprint for your life includes one very important and undeniable clause: All things are working together for your GOOD! So wipe that sweat off your brow and breathe! Whew!

On a side note, in the process of cleaning up 3 tons (no exaggeration here) of debris from the back yard, we unearthed an army of centipedes and slugs. I'm sure I was a sight

almost knocking people over, rushing for the salt, to vanquish a slug the size of Tokyo (I've included a pic!).

# KNOCKOUT TIME!

This morning when my eyes popped open in bed, I heard a voice in my mind say, "Round 3". How bizarre! Maybe it was because I had woken up an hour before and decided, "I want to sleep for another hour."  But then that would have made it Round 2. How weird.

I know I didn't imagine it, because the instant my eyes opened, I heard it. I didn't have a chance to catch a breath, or even think a thought. How peculiar. In my spirit, I know what it is. There has been a battle going on, in me and many of the people I know for a while. A battle that many will ignore, but I can't. The enemy is trying to wage a war... thing is, it's a war in which the outcome has already been determined. It's fixed. I WIN.

I WILL get EVERYTHING God says is mine in Jesus name. I had no dreams about boxing, no waking thoughts either, but if this morning's sunrise signals Round 3 then I'm ready. It's K.O. (knockout) time. See I have a line of defense. I may look little in the ring, like a pip squeak with a sling. But I have a secret weapon. My Rock, my Defender, my Strong Tower. THE MOST HIGH GOD. No, He's not in my corner... no Sir. He's above, around, before, behind, within and next to me. Mighty to save. The same one who championed the cross and ripped the keys of death, hell and the grave from Satan's slimy claws. Anything that dares to come in a ring with me has a date with the floor.

So here we go, Round 3! (Thank God I don't have to wear those funky looking boxing boots to do this!)

# A BRIDGE IS A BRIDGE IS A BRIDGE…

One day I got lost somewhere between the Bruckner and the Triborough. One is an expressway, the other is a bridge. I looked at all my doors and made sure all those little  manual door buttons were pressed down. Between trying to figure out if the sunglasses made my head pound more or less, I finally made a sharp right turn in the right direction. It was late. I was tired. I heard that now familiar reminder, "Round 3".

This time it wasn't the voice from earlier, it was the voice I recognize and love, Holy Spirit. "I know, I know", I checked myself and shook off my gloom. "They that wait upon the Lord shall renew their strength; they shall mount up with wings like eagles. They shall run and not grow weary; they shall walk and not faint."

All day yesterday as I nearly missed a speeding truck, wondered how all bridges basically look the same to me, found NO PLACE to park (not even in the last resort $13 garage) and sat alone in my room crying out to God, and His voice just reminded me: Round 3, and you win.

Below the cloak of battle though, lies the effervescent expectation of victory. I can't help but get excited when I remember that my Father God's eyes are constantly watching over me, working everything out for my good. I love where I am, in the center of His will!

# A STORM, A RAGING OCEAN AND ME...

The second my feet hit the ice cold surf I said, "Oh Jesus help me." I walked into the waves at Rockaway Beach with a friend in the rain. My goal was a perfect spot at a little over waist high, where I could comfortably immerse a 6 foot man. It was baptism day. The beach was closed and it's not the most brilliant of ideas to be in the water during a storm, but one of the candidates said, "Pastor if you don't baptize me today, I'm running into the water and baptizing myself."

As I tried to steady myself in about 3 1/2 feet of water, I looked to the left and saw a 3 footer wave approaching. Do the math. I jumped, got a slap in the face and settled back down on my feet. All the while, my friend, who is much taller, was grabbing my arms to make sure I didn't float away. A few moments later, in came Curt bringing with him, the first candidate, beaming from ear to ear. Because of the rain and the waves that had me soaked, no one could see that my eyes were filled with tears.

"Do you confess that Jesus Christ is the Lord of your life; that He died, was buried and rose again?" "Yes I do." He said, above the crash of the waves and the sound of the rain. "Then, upon the confession of your faith, I baptize you in the name of the Father, of the Son and of the Holy Spirit." And under he went.

You could hear the cheering on the beach as he sprung out of the water. Three more people took the plunge. By the time it was over and everyone had exited, I turned to look at the ocean and give thanks to the awesome God who created it. The rain felt warm and I was soaking; I felt like I, myself, had been baptized. I left renewed and exhilarated. Washed away with the ocean was fear, stress and exhaustion and in its place... the newness of life.

Have you been baptized? You know we are baptized into Christ's death and His resurrection? It is the place where we die. Die to the sin and past. It's the place where we say we are done with who we are and ready to be what God means for us to be. If you haven't done so yet... it's time.

# IN THE SHADOW OF HIS MIGHTY WINGS

I was lying on a wooden bench, in the shade of a huge tree, listening to the waves lap against the shore... right next to me... and listening to "The more I seek you" without my headphones.  I can't remember when I last felt this relaxed.  I was at a summer retreat in Texas and so far I was loving it...

Not too long ago, I remember sitting on my bed and asking God for a day by the water when I could just sit and watch the waves and talk to Him.  It was during that time when I left for work in the dark and came home in the dark.  As I lie there, He said, "Here we are."  That made my heart smile.

Undoubtedly, not all days will be as peaceful as this one and storms will certainly come, but in this moment I thank Him for the shelter of His mighty wings.  I thank Him, not just for the beauty His hands have made but because of who He is.

He is God, in my good times and bad, when I can't find a spot to park and when parking is the last thing on my mind. He is God when I'm blazin' a trail with His word and when I fail. He is God in my calm but He is GOD in my storm. He is my mountain moving, mighty to save, grave busting, soon coming King! He is God and He loves you and me.

Praise God from whom all blessings flow
Praise Him all creatures here below
Praise Him above, ye heavenly host
Praise Father, Son and Holy Ghost

# HOW DO YOU SPELL "EEEEK!"?

Oh the utter shame and horror! I cringe, as my fingers traverse this keyboard, at the very thought. An exterminator will visit my apartment today, and no, it's not for tea! A few days ago, while I was doing the dishes, something tiny scurried across the floor and caught my eye. I froze. Could it be? "Nah", I decided and finished up. To my intense dread, later that day, my friend confirmed my first suspicion: a baby roach. I have not yet seen the parent roach, but where there's a baby...

A week later and the roaches have a date with death. We've been in this apartment almost a year and had not seen a roach, and then suddenly, here they are. Did we leave crumbs on the floor? Dishes in the sink? These are the things that summon the vermin. "Or, it could be coming from the apartments next door", the super said.

Since I have no earthly desire to scrub my

neighbor's floors, I scrubbed mine to a hefty shine. I feel a cockroach running across them might be scared by his own reflection! If I didn't see the life lesson, you know I wouldn't be me... so here's my 2 cents.

We roll merrily along; day to day and never suspect that sin is creeping into our lives. It may not happen because of what we intentionally decide to do. It may be as a result of carelessness: harboring un-dealt-with pride, jealousy or unforgiveness. It may even creep in because of the influences of people we are with. But it always begins with a seemingly harmless and tiny action. No big deal.

The thing with sin and roaches, is that the tiny roach signals a potentially alarming condition: INFESTATION. One moment at a time, one complacent argument later (only this once) or one appeal (It's not that bad) and it's too late. On a side note, in the middle of the process of scrubbing everything in the house, the house looked like it contracted a virus: it looked like it kept throwing up on its self... Disastrous!

It was the process. Afterwards it is spotless. You get it. The cleanup is sometimes painful, but so worth it. It may look like its actually worsening rather than improving but it's the toughest part of the battle. "If we confess our sins, He is faithful and just to forgive us our sins and to cleanse us from all unrighteousness." 1 John 1:9 (KJV)

# WHAT DO YOU GET WHEN YOU CROSS AN OLD MAN WITH RANCH DRESSING?

On a flight back from Trinidad I was a bit concerned when I was sandwiched between an elderly gentleman (5C) and an even more elderly lady (5A). The thought of him having to shake me awake (I sleep on airplanes) to pass by on his way to the bathroom, or worse him falling asleep and stuff (like maybe teeth) falling out made me a bit nervous. He (5C) proved exactly like he seemed: mannerly and serious in his impressive dark blue blazer. The little lady on the other hand, insisted on pushing the flight attendant call button every five minutes, and grabbing the arm of the attendant and pulling her down till her face was in front of her little old lady glasses to ask for a glass of water. It was hilarious.

Things moved merrily along and the old lady told me, "You take care of me better than the waitress." I thought, "Lord please don't let her call the flight attendant a waitress." Merrily along that is, until they served a meal. It was somewhat awkward because the old man in 5C in the impressive blazer didn't look like the friendliest type. In fact, he refused the meal and pulled out his own non-fat yogurt, granola bar and juice! "Aren't you at least going to take the Twix?" I asked him and behind his polite "No" I saw a hint of a smile... just a hint because he promptly proceeded to ignore me again.

I picked up my sealed cup of ranch dressing and was wrestling with the on-too-tightly peel-off cover. I tugged and tugged and it finally flew off, along with a spray of ranch dressing... all over 5C's dark blue blazer! Oh the utter horror! I looked at his face and to my surprise; he had no idea that his navy blue blazer was now a navy-blue-with-white-polka dots blazer.

 I actually thought, in a moment of weakness, "Maybe I shouldn't say anything and act surprised when he notices." My reflexes kicked in before the end of the thought and before I knew it I was poking, jabbing and swabbing him with paper towels. "I am so sorry; I got this all over you!" I lamented. He turned to face me. He looked straight in my eyes. I looked as apologetic as I could. He smiled. "Don't worry about it. This has to go to the cleaners anyway." Hallelujah!

For the rest of the trip we talked about why he

should get an iPhone and I showed him and 5A lady pictures of Curt and my nieces and nephews. In baggage claim, 5A lady insisted that I introduce her to Curt and she hugged him like she knew him. Then out of the corner of my eye, I saw a bright smile and a huge wave from 5C in the blue blazer. Praise God His mercies are still new every morning!

# I WEIGH WHAT???

"Honey, something's wrong with this scale!" I screamed as I looked down on the bright green numbers flashing between my feet. There is just no way I gained that much weight since moving to New York. It's like I not only moved to the Big Apple, I dipped it in caramel, rolled it in sprinkles and ate it.

That was the peak of my surprise meter. Now that the realization has become less of a myth and more of a reality of my body's betrayal... I'm drinking more water. I almost dash by the bathroom so I don't see the scale monster. If I must, I approach it like a timid swimmer dipping his toe in the freezing pool before going in. I watch the numbers rise and I'm more surprised at how, surprised I am at the numbers I read. "No way!" I hear my mind say, "Nooo way Jose!"

It strikes me that if that is what I am most concerned about in life I may be one of two things: 1) a hermit or 2) clueless. Amidst the world of websites that find husbands AND serial killers, excessive greed, murders of unborn children, and the abuse of many that are born, economic vomiting, Kanye's verbal vomiting and a host of other maladies, a few extra pounds seems too trivial to base a piece on.

So this cannot necessarily be about my weight, but rather the host of inconsequential's that we put so much weight on every day. That $1 raise we didn't get, that new makeup that we can't afford, that car, that house, that fluffy toilet seat cover. Or even, who hurt me and made me cry last Thursday, not last but the Thursday before the one before, the guy who said I said, when I really didn't say, the girl who did me wrong when all I did was care for them, the perfect stranger that peed in my cornflakes (pardon the language). I think we should really, no seriously friends, really just let it go.

Life is too short and there is too much important stuff to do to keep wallowing in the mud of self pity. So, am I getting on the scale again? Maybe tomorrow or the day after because today I'm taking the stairs!

# HURRY UP ALREADY!

With October peeking slyly around the corner, I thought it the perfect time to start getting ready. We're having a couples conference soon and I've been devouring scripture and other recommended reading in preparation for the event. Well, I'm stuck.

As much as I abhor the admittance, I'm stuck in a book... the first chapter to be precise. It is now my 3rd successive day of re-reading said chapter. The Book: The Love Dare. The chapter: 1. See, herein lies my dilemma: At the end of every chapter, there is a "dare" that the reader performs, and a box you "check" when the dare is completed.

The authors of the book were utterly cunning when they made the first chapter, "Love is Patient". I know what you're thinking, "That's what it says and how it's said in the bible." and you would be right. After so many years of marriage to the same wonderful, painfully patient person, I have come to appreciate the virtue and recognize my deficiency thereof. Here is the dare: For the next day resolve to demonstrate patience and to say NOTHING NEGATIVE TO YOUR SPOUSE AT ALL.

See what I mean? "That's not hard to do Sharo!" I hear your "speck-in-the-eye" assessment. And again, you're right... unless you were me driving down a New York road in the middle of the Bronx with your flat tire light flashing wickedly from the dashboard. Calm down Sharo, I warned myself, just don't say anything negative. I dialed,

"Honey, my tire is going flat, I'm at Castle Hill and I can't see any gas stations to get air."
"OK. Where are you?"
"Ummm... Castle Hill" I replied again. (10 points for patience)
"Alright then, listen, just turn right on to Castle Hill and before you get to the Whitestone there is a Mobile right there." he said with a 'you've passed there a million times before' tone.
"I'm already on Castle Hill Honey."
"Oh, Ok then. If you are already on Castle Hill then it should be right there babe."
"Right where?"... Still doing well.
"Listen, as soon as you turn on to Castle Hill Avenue, make a right and at the light a left, it's right there!"
Sigh, "I'm not on Castle Hill anymore." (Still patient and positive)
Now he's a little more assertive, "Honey you must have passed straight by the gas station."
"Well you took too long to tell me!" BUSTED!

There was the negative, spewing and vomited out before I could stop it. I apologized quickly and hung up and resolved to start again. So today is day four of the patience dare. Curtis thinks it's funny, me: not so much. I am resolved however, to finish the dare and indeed, the book. I just wish I could hurry up and get past the first chapter on patience! "Be completely humble and gentle; be patient, bearing with one another in love." Ephesians 4:2 (NIV)

# CHICAGO IN NEW YORK... SORT OF

There's this sappy old song by Chicago that goes,
"You're the meaning in my life, you're the
inspiration. You bring meaning to my life... You're
the ins..."

You know the song. Well I was shamelessly
bellowing it out at the top of my lungs with the radio,
as I crossed the Hudson in my little red Chevy this
morning. (I know, I'm giving my age away) Even
amidst my milk-curdling chords, I snatched a quick
glimpse of the city to my left and then the deep aqua
billows to the right... and predictably, my breath got
caught in my throat and my chin almost hit the
steering wheel. The beauty almost always robs me of
my breath.

Still driving, hands now at 10 and 2, I glanced
quickly upward to the most picturesque and
breathtaking view of the sky. "WOW!" Today I
tipped my proverbial hat to the ONE who with just a

word, created the cosmos and the millions of stars in this galaxy and the millions of galaxies never seen. As tears soaked with adoration, stained my cheeks, my heart bowed itself in reverence to the One who designed, implemented and still orchestrates it all. Without a thought further and without meditated notions of any description, I felt my soul cry out: "Even so... come Lord Jesus!"

While my heart aches today for the thousands in Indonesia who have lost families and loved ones in an earthquake this week, and I am miserable with longing to help the dying in Samoa, struck by a violent Tsunami again this week... I selfishly pine tonight for the face of the One who first loved me.

God willing, one day I will be Hope to the victims of disasters in ways other than sincere prayer, but today when prayer is what I have to give... I ask my Abba to bring comfort to those who mourn. To know Jesus is to always have a hope and assurance. I recognize that this week, many people sailed past the boundaries of mere human existence and woke up face to face with the One True God: my Abba.

I passed the toll booth and bellowed like the kid chasing the departing ice-cream truck with a renewed vigor. He is undeniably, unequivocally and utterly... my inspiration. "You should know, everywhere I go, you're always on my mind, in my heart, in my soul. You're the meaning in my life, you're the inspiration..."

Update: In 2012, Hurricane Sandy hit New York

and just as I prayed on this day so many years before, God let me bring "Hope" to thousands of people. Over 2 million bottles of water, 400,000 family meals, 800,000 winter coats and so much more were distributed from HopeNYC church to every borough in New York. He is such an amazing God.

# THE CHICKEN NUGGETS MADE ME
# CRY

The chicken nuggets made me cry. I love New York because that's where God wants me to be at this point in my life, I love the people that He has put in my path and am utterly excited by the future He has mapped out for me. A 3 day hop into Houston though reminded me of the joys I've left behind.

The three year old girl that said , "But aunty can you stay one more day?", the large rooms, large buffets at tiny prices, real dollar stores, clean streets and abundant smiles from people you've never seen before and may never see again... stir me.

On the way to the airport we stopped in at a Chic-Fil-A. We opened the door into what seemed like fast food heaven. It looked brand new even though it wasn't. We were greeted by a tall manager guy with a beaming smile and friendly voice, "Good morning guys." I shoved the disbelief and cynical "What's wrong with these people?" to the back of my mind and soaked in with appreciation, the true southern hospitality I already find myself forgetting. By the time the little guy behind the cash register took my mini chicken biscuits (made with chicken breast- no

parts- meat, cooked in 100% peanut oil which is naturally cholesterol and saturated fat free) order and smiled warmly as he talked about the weather being a smudge warmer in Texas than New York, my eyes were brimming.

My sister-in-law looked at me in disbelief while my husband with pleading "Don't embarrass me!" eyes, just stood there. It wasn't just the kindness and the lack of next-customer-in-line NY abruptness, it wasn't just the "How may I help you?" sincerity of ALL the employees we met there or the clean and spacious restaurant, but it was the gratitude in my heart that God let me spend more than a decade in Houston and now took me to a place I love more than I ever thought I could love a place. It is the thankfulness in my heart to Him for letting me be able to visit and the way I hear His voice saying, "I love you" in the things I sometimes take for granted.

Now I'm on an airplane back to New York. Hundreds of feet below my window I see a floor of puffy clouds and a beautiful horizon in the distance. I simply can't wait to see where God takes me in this life... But I promise you I am thoroughly enjoying the journey. There are those brimming eyes again. "How marvelous are your works Oh Lord." The chicken nuggets at that Chic-Fil-A were wonderful!

## BUBBLE POPPING PARTY TIME!

Sometimes my stomach tightens and I look

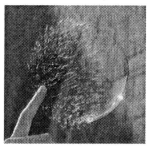

around, out of the corner of my eyes, weird smile on my face, almost suspicious of myself for being this peaceful. Really, the woman I was a half a decade ago was way more expressive, emotional and erratic. About now I'd be a smidge panicky because there's so much to do and so little time to do it in. Now... there's still so much to do, less time to do it in, and my heart is at peace.

In fact, the stomach tightening feeling is because I feel just a touch of guilt for feeling this calm, when a more appropriate scenario would be to run in circles, stomp invisible ants and pop floating bubbles. I feel like maybe I should be, but NO. My new home looks like WW3 has erupted within the confines of its walls, and all the ammunition we have are boxes of things and bags of clothes. The war was brutal, it was a massive raid: stuff is everywhere.

Yesterday I skated on my backside dragging a 150 pound box of anatomy books down the hall. I surrendered at the half way point and abandoned it there. I have the bruises and battle scars. The only thing that hurts is when I look at the TV stand I allen-wrenched, screwdrivered and hammered together, all by myself and I notice that the front doors are a bit lopsided. I'm blaming the floors! I love my new home. Thank you Jesus!

More than that though, the stomach tightening is because it's Christmas at Hope. It's so busy and beautiful I love it! I love this season and it has nothing to do with the presents and EVERYTHING to do with the people. God has blessed my life with the most wonderful people. My husband, family, relatives, friends, congregation... really shine in my life... especially at times like these. So today I thank God with all my heart. All those people make this "WW3" a stomach tightening, weird smiling, ant stomping, bubble popping an amazing journey!

# I'M STARTING TODAY!

The new decade is rolling merrily along and January is actually almost over. It's been a while since I sat down to write this way and I missed it. In the epic salutation of God's peace however, "Fear not"... I was writing. Though no blog... for the past few weeks I joined in fasting with hundreds of thousands of Christ followers all over this planet and I journaled my journey.

Today however, is not about that. Today is the day I put on my deciding hat and resolve to accomplish. Accomplish what? Well... whatever I want actually. No it's not New Years Day. It's not my Birthday. I didn't have an epiphany this morning...

See... this morning I have a brand new set. Not chess, not chores and not teeth... but mercies. That means I have no less than I did on New Year's Day or any day since My Savior died for me.

Consequently, today is a perfect day for me to resolve to accomplish. I resolve to start my next book this year, love people more, work harder at being a better wife, pastor, daughter, sister, aunt, friend; eat better but enjoy the things I love more, keep off the 20 odd pounds I lost during this fast and a few other things.

I get a strong sense of new beginnings today... and I appreciate it. I resolve to not punish myself if I struggle to meet my own expectations, because today I remember that God's ample chest is always there for me to rest my head on.

The small beam of sunlight dancing across my keyboard is helping me remember that He is in charge. Yesterday it felt like some giant was power washing the streets of Queens and I was the grasshopper caught in it with my umbrella. At least twice I was almost airborne. But today the sun is shining and the gusts have gone to other streets. So I'm resolving.

What are your plans for this year? What if this is the year of our Lord's return? How are you "occupying" till He comes?

# THE FATHER'S GOOD PLEASURE

Meditate on: Phil 4:19

What do you need this morning? Our meditation scripture reads, "My God shall supply ALL your needs according to His riches in glory." I choose today to take that at face value. I'm not going into a long discussion between the differences between needs and wants. I'm also not going to go on about the abundance of riches at God's disposal and how meaningless the stuff we crave is to Him. That, you already know. Today, instead, I want to remind you that He shall and He wants to. Not only does He say He will but He wants to supply your needs. He also says, "Fear not little flock, for it is the Father's good pleasure to give you the kingdom." Luke 12:32 (KJV)

So now, it is up to you to cast off all that heaviness that sits on your shoulders, all that wondering whether or not the Lord WANTS to bless. It is HIS PLEASURE, HE said to give us righteousness, peace and joy in the Holy Ghost. Just as a father pities his children, so much more does our Father pity them that fear Him. That word "pitieth" does not come across as clearly in our language as it did in the original. The actual word is "racham" which means love or compassion. He loves you and feels for you in the deepest part of Him. God feels for you in His proverbial "gut". Imagine that... He is moved by your cries and He hears you.

So take it to heart today, come boldly to His throne and make your requests known. He is your Abba Father, your daddy God. Take the time to speak with Him, one on one, Father and son.

# THE SPIRIT KNOWS

Rom 8:28-(NLT) "And we know that God causes everything to work together for the good of those who love God and are called according to his purpose for them."

See if you get this:

**What He knows:** the mind of the Spirit, (so He intercedes on our behalf... asking for the things the Spirit knows we need, though we may not.)

**What We know:** that ALL things are working together for our good.

Thank GOD that the Spirit knows about me, what I don't know about me. I think I know what I need in my life. I have however, lived long enough to know that what I think I want today, or need, may be vastly different tomorrow. That's why, I suspect, the

Psalmist says, "Search me Oh God and know my heart, try me and know my thoughts." When the Spirit searches your spirit, and knows what is best, He sets a plan in motion in your life that may throw you for a loop.

GOD explained to us that the way we would take and the thoughts we think are vastly different from His. Yet He "knows," He is fully aware of His plans for you.

"I don't understand Lord. How could you let this happen?" we cry out honestly. We cry because all we see is our present circumstance, like a little ant in a maze. All you know is that there is a big wall in front of you, but God is watching over you and your tiny maze and sees the whole picture. He sees the end and knows that if you follow His voice, you will come out perfectly.

So no matter the situation, I hold fast to what I know. I know He knows.

# YOU ARE LOVED

I love the Lord.
That's me, by definition.
Everything I am stems from that declaration.

I love the ocean because it reminds me of His majesty. I love sunrises, the sound of rain and the changing seasons because they speak of His creativity. I love Christmas, because it's all about Him. I love good friends, great food and fun times because He gave me the breath to enjoy them. I love my family; He chose them just for me. I love my husband, he reminds me of HIM. Today I thought at length of His wonderful goodness. He, the majestic King of Heaven, takes the time to think about Sharo... wow!

He takes the time to think about you my friend. He loves you so much that He has written your name on His palms. Does that make you say "wow"? It amazes me.

Sometimes I write a "C and S" on my nail because it  reminds me of how happy I am to have Curtis in my life (see pic). It's something I did before we were married and still I do it, after 20 years of marriage. Your name is on Jehovah's hand. WOW.

Let's take some precious moments today to love Him intimately, to tell Him how wonderful He is. He is the Holy One, the Lord of Hosts, the One True God and He cares for you. Know that you are His beloved. I can't tell you all the reasons why He loves you so... I just know He does.

# STILL WAITING

Ever got stuck waiting before? I'm not only  talking about waiting on God here. I'm talking about waiting on a taxi to pick you up, waiting on that promotion, waiting for dinner to be ready or waiting for your chance to get the remote control? Nobody likes to wait. At least we don't want to wait for what we want. Today I'm not going to talk you into waiting, I'll just suggest that while you do... looking for the moving of God... that you "Forget not all His benefits." You have an advocate, defender and Savior that is always in your corner. And what magnificent benefits they are. Heaven is your eternal home. Almighty God is your Abba Father.

When I was a younger wife, I would always set

myself up. When Curt was a little late coming from work, I would never, to my great sorrow, assume the obvious. I wouldn't think, "He's stuck in traffic" or "was detained at work" or "stopped at the gas station." No, I would think, "He's late because he stopped to buy me flowers." Then when my exhausted husband walked through the doors empty handed, no flowers, I felt so let down. He could never understand why and I was too embarrassed to divulge that. I had worked myself into a frenzy of expectation. But then there were those days when he would leave for work and return a half hour later, flowers in hand, or send me 120 roses on our anniversary, and completely overwhelm me.

Sometimes we work ourselves into a tizzy expecting God to answer our prayers in the ways we expect. But His ways are so very far from ours, and His thoughts are so very different. When He works, it is better than we expected and beyond our hopes. So why not let Him work. Stop crying about His process and how long, or painful or disappointing it seems and trust that He is working things out for your good.

My soul is satisfied, for as the heaven is high above the earth, [so] great is his mercy toward them that fear him.

# FAST WITH PURPOSE

After a 21 day Fast you step over into breakthrough territory. The kind of place that Joel talked about in chapter 2 and that Paul talked about in Acts chapter 2. Friends I cannot stress enough to you the urgency of the time we live in. We are standing on a planet that is orbiting into its own demise, because the homo sapiens that walk it, think somehow, that they are smart enough to decide whether or not God exists... bad idea. He is not subject to our opinions neither is His glory affected by our ignorance. He is God.

Our country maybe whirling to a Godless, ethicless and corrupt land mass of economic and moral chaos... but somewhere in New York, in Africa, in Trinidad, in the UK, in Canada, there was a man, woman, boy or girl falling on their face before God. For 21 days you give more of yourself to Him than ever before and you see the results of your obedience and sacrifice. Expect your miracle. Faith is the substance of things hoped for, the evidence of things not seen. You will see what a mighty God you serve. All your pain, sickness, sorrow and sin, was already borne by Him, for the Lord had laid on Him the iniquity of us all.

More than anything… focus on the wonderful CROSS. That old rugged cross where Jesus freely laid down His life so that we'd have a chance at eternal life... I cherish that cross. Let us thank Him that because of His blood that flowed down, our sins are washed away today, our names are written in the Lamb's book of Life and we are no longer slaves to sin. We are God's and He is ours!

# THIS IS FOR YOU

Of all the things I can do for you today, the least effective would be to worry about you. I know things are not everything you wish they were, I know there are things you would change, and I know I can't change them for you. I could call you and tell you to hold on, and that would mean something to you perhaps. I could send you a card in the mail, to let you know that God is still your Father. I could text you to see if you're keeping out of trouble and watch you like a pit bull to make sure you don't forfeit your blessing. I could send a message with a friend to make sure you don't think I'm mad at you. And send a balloon-a-gram to make sure you're not mad at me.

But worry is worthless. Balloons deflate. Cards take too long and e-mails are so impersonal. All of those things are sometimes necessary... but can I do that for you every week? Every day? Every minute? Is that the relationship we have?

But God remembers you today. Today the Son intercedes before the Father for you, again. If I could, I would ask Him to answer your prayers, heal your hurt, shorten your waiting, dispel your anxiety and correct your misunderstandings. I'd even ask Him to lead you away from temptation and protect you from evil. I'd probably cry to Him for your sake, and you may not even cry for your own. Today I will pray that my Father in heaven will be touched by my heart that is breaking for you, and He will bless you.

I can't explain to you that there is no one person in my heart this morning, but you. You, who are reading this page, are looking for God to show up for you. As you read this, know that I spent time, face to the earth, before the throne today for you that would read this. Be blessed.

# MOVING STRAIGHT FORWARD

Isaiah 43:14-19 (NLT)

[14] This is what the LORD says-your Redeemer, the Holy One of Israel: "For your sakes I will send an army against Babylon, forcing the Babylonians to flee in those ships they are so proud of. [15] I am the LORD, your Holy One, Israel's Creator and King. [16] I am the LORD, who opened a way through the waters, making a dry path through the sea. [17] I called forth the mighty army of Egypt with all its chariots and horses. I drew them beneath the waves, and they drowned, their lives snuffed out like a smoldering candlewick. [18] "But forget all that- it is nothing compared to what I am going to do. [19] For I am about to do something new. See, I have already begun! Do you not see it? I will make a pathway through the wilderness. I will create rivers in the dry wasteland."

Today as you meditate on His word, there is a verse in today's reading that speaks loudly to me: vs. 18 "But forget all that- it is nothing compared to what

I am going to do." Now stop and read that again and again until you feel that in your soul. (I read it 16 times)

Hear the word of God to His people. Previously in this chapter, the Lord had been recounting to the Israelites through Isaiah, all the mighty works and miracles He had done for them. He reminded them of the Red Sea, and that He brought them through the fire, He took them through the wilderness and rescued them from tyranny... He brought all His wonderful miracles to their attention so that they would remember that He is GOD.

He wants us to remember His goodness. All of His many benefits and blessings that we enjoy are because of His love and mercy for us. As we remember, let us recognize that He is GOD and He is Holy. If you're journaling, take a moment to write those down, as many as you can. Recall God's goodness in your life. Then read vs. 18 again: "But forget all that- it is nothing compared to what I am going to do."

What a word! Now that you've remembered... forget it... because it doesn't even compare to what's ahead! Then He goes on to say, "For I am about to do something new. See I have already begun! Do you not see it?"

It is mind writing to think about what God can possibly do for me that's bigger than what He's already done... and then He says "See... Do you not see it?" My friend, His word says in 1Cor 2:9-10 (NKJ) "But as it is written, Eye hath not seen, nor ear heard, neither have entered into the heart of man, the things which God hath prepared for them that love him. But God hath revealed [them] unto us by his Spirit: for the Spirit searcheth all things, yea, the deep things of God."

If we follow the Holy Spirit, whichever way He leads us, He reveals what God has prepared for us and leads us straight to it. No chicken leg is worth giving that up for! Let this word from God light a Holy fire in you, motivate you to pursue Him and encourage you to enjoy reading the word. You've taken the right step today... Straight Forward.

# COMB YOUR HAIR AND WASH YOUR FACE

Pray like this:
Our Father in heaven,
May your name be kept holy.
May your Kingdom come soon.
May your will be done on earth,
As it is in heaven.
Give us today the food we need,
and forgive us our sins,
As we have forgiven those who sin against us.
And don't let us yield to temptation,
But rescue us from the evil one.
"If you forgive those who sin against you, your
heavenly Father will forgive you.
But if you refuse to forgive others, your Father will
not forgive your sins."

In Matthew chapter 6, Jesus provides the 3 "must
do's" and spoke to us of them as if they were

understood. He says, "When you pray" "When you give" and "When you fast." None of these have an "if" attached to them. It is the understood duty of the Christian to pray, to give and to fast. Most of us have no trouble with the praying and giving... it's the fasting part that stomps us.

I believe that when we practice all these disciplines, we release the faith that substantiate the blessings that Jesus talks about in Mark 4, blessings that are 30, 60 and 100 fold returns. One out of three or two out of three are not obedience, because obedience is not measured in degrees. You either "are" or you "aren't". If this kind of return is elusive, maybe you have been missing one of the major components of your spiritual life: fasting.

It is also important that as we fast, we do not constantly gripe and complain so that the world pities us, and we pity ourselves. If we are doing this to honor Him who loved us, to ask His favor and follow His example, then let us do so with as much grace as we can muster.

You may find yourself wondering "What did I get myself into?" The flesh that you live in is in rebellion against the deprivation and denial of fasting and succumbing to a scrap of bread feels more like Christmas than just a feeble temptation. Don't give in. What you feel is your flesh submitting to your spirit... and it isn't happy. So today I would like to remind you of WHY we should fast:

• Fasting releases the anointing, the favor and the

blessings of God upon a believer's life.  Do you want more of these?  I DO!  What is that breakthrough in your life that you need?  Fasting and prayer will bring it!

• Every major biblical figure including Jesus, fasted.  Our example to follow is our Lord, and if He, the Son of God, felt the need to fast and did it often... then who are we? (Matt 4)

• As your mind and body becomes uncluttered with the pollutants and toxins of this world, your Spirit will become more sensitive to God. (Is 26:3)

• Fasting will rid your body of toxins and impurities and the result will be a healthier you.  Do you need that? (1Chr 6:19)

• Fasting puts the devil to flight.  Jesus told His disciples that certain spirits will not leave except by fasting and prayer. (Matt. 17:20-21)[1]

These are just a small number of the many reasons why we should fast.

When I was about 4 years old I watched my Godmother and parents fast, and I really wanted to do it as well. I would try to fast for a day.  I started off really strongly and by noon, I would give up. Every year however I would last a little bit longer.  I remember the first time I fasted the entire day... I was 7 years old and I spent most of the day scouring

---

[1] Jentzen Franklin *Fasting*

around for stuff to eat when my fast ended. Hopefully, this is not where you find yourself during a fast. Now when we fast for 21 days it is a privilege for me because I am well aware of the miracles that are born out of these fasts!

# HAPPY BIRTHDAY DARLING

 I can't tell you yet, what I got him for his birthday, because he hasn't seen it yet. I'll let you know later. I don't know when last I've been this excited to give someone a gift. I know it's more than he expects, because I have been planning this for a while. He will be so amazed!! I can hardly stand it! Today is Curt's birthday.

I'm celebrating the day that God chose to bring Curtis Ramkhelawan in to the world. His parents looked at him and saw their baby boy. They had no idea about the life that was ahead of him. They didn't know that when he was just 9 years old, Curt would lose his dad to leukemia. They didn't know that he would be dealt another blow at 15, and lose his mom as well. I don't know if they would have made different choices if they knew that he would have to be a father to his 3 sisters.

But if I could see them, I'd tell them he did a wonderful and amazing job. He took care of their daughters, he built them a nice house, and he worked every day since he was a teenager to make sure they were taken care of. He gave up things so that they would be happy. He takes care of me. He still gives up things to make me happy.

Today I'm excited to give Him this gift because I know he'll love it... and I feel like crying. This makes me think about my first love... My LORD... when I come to His house to offer Him a gift. How much thought, effort, and love do I put into my gift... Of praise... Of offering. Am I trembling at the thought of His face when He sees it? Or do I just slap it down carelessly... not caring about how it makes Him feel?

Oh God... my desire is to give You all... everything I have, I am, I can do... ALL.... with great anticipation of the look on Your face... the smile of a God who loves the gift and first loved the giver.

# YOU'RE SO GLIB!

 What's more intense than a good game of scrabble? Ok, ok... maybe scrabble is not the most adrenalin-pumping "sport" in the world, but I still like to win. So in my last scrabble game I made the word "glib". My opponent laughed so hard, I thought he might burst a blood vessel. In fact he was almost to the point of tears!

"Glib? Glib? What's glib?" he kept remarking through annoying guffaws and shrieking laughter. "Glib", I answered, "You know, like in 'you're so glib." That just made him laugh louder and harder. In fact he was laughing so much that I began to doubt myself. I was getting ready to scrap the word.

My opponent was so sure that he was right that he

insisted on looking up the word in the dictionary. Here's what he found:

glib: Pronunciation: \'glib\

Function: adjective: marked by ease and informality; nonchalant
b: showing little forethought or preparation
c: lacking depth and substance

Oh the taste of Victory! He was shocked. I knew that was a word. I was elated. You know, it's not just the truth, but it's the-truth-you-know that sets you free. Truth remains just that, whether we choose to subscribe to it, deny it or ignore it. Or maybe I should say "Him". Jesus said, "I am the way, the TRUTH and the Life." That truth still sets men free and whoever He sets free is free indeed! If you already know the truth, really know Him, no one can take that from you. I heard someone say, denying the truth never negates its existence.

By the way... I won the game!

# MY SIX-PACK!

Last night I set my alarm early for this very purpose. I woke up at the ringing and headed straight to the kitchen. Drank my juicy vitamin and bee-lined to the DVD player. Popped in my amazing DVD and tried to psych myself up for 20 minutes of body-shaping, abs-forming, fat-burning, muscle toning goodness!

Two and a half minutes later I was lying on my couch contentedly watching the people on the TV screen sweat up a storm. And 8, 7, 6, 5, 4... I even counted along. I find that when I do a bit of exercise in the morning, I'm more alert, energetic and sharp during the day. I work harder, pray longer, read more, think clearer not to mention work on that 6-pack and stay in shape... but not even the knowledge of those incredible benefits was motivation enough to get me off my gluteus maximus this morning.

I sit here now, fully aware that watching the

exercise DVD did not benefit my body... in fact the only thing that got a work out were the muscles in my eyes. Listening to other people talk about God and even watching them do His will without putting that word into practice ourselves, is similarly futile. There is no impact on our spiritual lives. In fact we can sit there and watch others all we want... and even convince ourselves that we're at least doing some good. But the truth is that Good Intentions are not Good Enough... Not at all.

After all "Faith without works is dead" James 2:20 So... that said... what do you think I'll be doing tomorrow morning? I'll tell you. I'm putting that DVD in the closet and I'm riding my bike to work. James 2:18 (NIV) But someone will say, "You have faith; I have deeds." Show me your faith without deeds, and I will show you my faith by what I do.

# TALKING PUNKY... MY DOG

 I have a dog. His name is Punky. He is a long haired Chihuahua. Even though it seems I have always had a pet and I've loved each one, I am by-no-means the biggest animal aficionado. The thought of animals being in captivity, makes me sad. The thought of being chased by a wild boar makes me sadder though. The elephants at the circus rearing up on hind legs, balancing their heavy bodies at the crack of a man's whip drag me to a somber melancholy at the thought of such overwhelming creatures in such underwhelming circumstance.

Punky doesn't inspire that in me. I'm happy to see him when I return home because he grins his doggy mouth into a smile and wags his tail so ferociously I think one day he'll hover like a helicopter. Then in another breath, I want to banish him to an SPCA in the sky because he "left his mark" on another piece of my furniture. But he's my puppy.

Balaam had a pet too: a female donkey. Let's call her Eliza. Eliza was his pet as well as his mode of transportation (like many guys and their cars!). An angry angel stood in the middle of the road with a sword. Balaam did not see him but Eliza did. She immediately veered off the road and dove into a field (perhaps similar to what I might have done). Then, "Balaam beat her to get her back on the road." In fact, he beat her three times.

Poor Eliza... But get this: Suddenly Eliza… yes the donkey, starts talking! "What did I do to you for you to be beating up on me?" Wow. If Punky ever looked at me and said anything but "bark bark", I don't know how long I'd remain conscious.

But Balaam did something even stranger… he answered the donkey. He threatened to kill her. It was his own blindness that prevented him from seeing the angel. A simple animal could see but he couldn't and that made him mad at her. It wasn't her fault, just like it's not anyone else's fault when we are blind to God and His will. It's OUR fault... no one else's. We can point fingers at others for the lack of anointing, blessing and joy in our lives… but that's sillier than holding an English debate with your pet dog... and the dog winning.

Instead of looking for a place to lay blame, let's claim the blame. Repent. Change. I ask God to open my eyes to see Him, manifesting in my life in whatever way He pleases.  I want to see you Lord.

Meanwhile, I'm keeping a close eye on that Chihuahua of mine.  I heard him snoring.  I first thought it was Curt... but it was Punky.  Snoring is OK... just as long as he's not talking!

# HELP! WE'VE BEEN ROBBED!!

One night, in a good part of town, we were burglarized. By "we" I mean Curtis and I and by "burglarized" I mean someone broke the window of my car and got in and stole my purse. I know what you're thinking... "Sharo, why did you leave your purse in the car?" Well that's the beauty about hindsight: it's 20/20.

Even though my purse was under the mat and covered with a jacket... it was still stolen, along with my driver's license, S.S. card, credit cards, keys and other valuables. Curt and I were coming back from what was an awesome night out, and it was the coldest night of the year. We were parked along a very poorly lit street along with other cars and I was more than eager to get in and out of the cold. As we approached the car and I saw what was left of my broken window I thought it was ice for a few seconds... before I realized the truth.

About an hour and a half later, we had filed a report and talked with others on the street that had also been robbed. On the way home there was nothing we could do to keep the wind out... because a window was missing. We were thanking God that worse hadn't happened. Someone had lost their entire car (the beauty of having a car nobody really wants LOL).

Through the whole thing it was hard not to feel negligent or somehow responsible that someone broke into our car and invaded our space. We left a "door open" as it were... and the thieves came in. Do we leave ourselves open and vulnerable to the devil in the same way? Do we guard our integrity, honor and soul with diligence? Do we think that everything is OK and harmless when all the while we're tempting the enemy to take a stab at us? "Stuff" is replaceable but the enemy of our souls is interested in our permanent loss. God came so that we will have abundant life though... and the God in us is greater than the enemy out there! I will definitely be more careful, with my actions and "property" but more so, with God's property: ME.

# HOT PINK EARPLUGS AND A ZIT...

The first thing I did when I woke up this morning was open my eyes. Curt was praying and saying a blessing over me... and I was getting ready to hit the snooze button. My hot pink earplugs were a bit uncomfortable and since the husband and the doggy were now both awake, I took them out. I shut my eyes again and tried to drift back into the dream I had left unresolved... to no avail. I couldn't fall back asleep.

I thought about how cushy my soft blankets felt and how I didn't have a single pain anywhere in my body and as I felt my left cheek I thought about how terrific it was that the little zit I feared would appear this morning, never did. As the cogs, wheels and bearings of my consciousness geared up to face the day, my mind took off at top speed. Wondering, calculating, devising, organizing, planning, remembering... and then I heard something. Like a voice of a tiny child that is just waking up... I heard the sound of my own heart.

At the risk of sounding melodramatic, I'll tell you just like I felt it. My heart was searching for the one thing that makes it beat. It was the cry of longing. The one you feel when you're waiting at the airport to see someone you love get off the airplane... someone you haven't seen for a long time.

Even though my mind took off on its own course, my heart was longing for God. That's why God looks at the heart. It's the part of us that longs most for communion with him. I gathered my frenzied thoughts and put them into a miniature space at the back of my mind, to think about the One who gave me another welcome breath.

Suddenly it made sense again, why David said "my heart cries out for you" and "early in the morning I'll wake up and look for You." Before the Pilates, 5 servings of fruit and the first look at that morning face that only a mother, husband and God could love, we take a moment to look to the face of our mighty God. Gaze into the beauty of the most magnificent and incredible wonder of the world... now and to come. What a way to start a day!

# AMMM... THERE'S SOMETHING IN YOUR TEETH…

Ammm... there's something in your teeth.  Oh the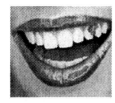 utter mortification!  You look in the mirror after spending an hour in the face of your friends to see a colorful piece of your dinner stuck in your teeth.  Ever happened to you?  I dare say all spinach eaters have faced this torture.  Why didn't they tell me? Gosh!  How could they let me walk around looking like an idiot?  They probably didn't want to embarrass me...

Truth be told though, it's far more embarrassing to walk around, laughing out loud, with a chunk of cheese in your teeth, than it is to quietly pick it out after your friend says, "Sharo... you have something stuck right there…"

We say nothing to spare our friends' feelings.

But... wouldn't you rather be told? I would. In a private, non-confrontational, friendly, quiet way... like true friends do it. True friends will let you know when you're setting yourself up. They will discreetly point out what you can fix... in love and truth... all the while being aware that the chunk in their teeth is probably bigger! "Sometimes we can see the splinter in our friend's eye and not the light pole in ours."

So let's decide to take and give constructive criticism in the right way and for the right reasons and in a timely manner. Friends don't let friends get so caught up in sin that they can't get out. Because we love each other... OR ... maybe one day "Chunky teeth will be in style!" I hope not.

Ephesians 4:15 (Amplified Bible)
[15] let our lives lovingly express truth [in all things, speaking truly, dealing truly, and living truly. Enfolded in love, let us grow up in every way and in all things into Him Who is the Head, [even] Christ (the Messiah, the Anointed One).

# A MIRACLE FOR YOU...

Before you ever said a prayer, read your bible or believed in faith... GOD DID A MIRACLE FOR YOU. We see all the miracles in the bible and hear of all the miracles in our church and we think about how great and wonderful that GOD would perform them. But every great prophet responded to the same miracle available to you today: that is the miracle of being able to know God. Your God is the ONE TRUE GOD, who has made Himself available to His creation. No other god humbled himself, far less to the point of death. Jehovah has given us the keys to knowing Him. He encourages us to seek and we will find Him, to pursue His presence, know His ways and even tells us plainly: they that worship Me must worship Me in Spirit and in truth.

The prophet Elijah is considered one of the most dramatic of the prophets for his exploits and miracles. He predicted the beginning and ending of drought in Israel, raised the dead, was fed by ravens and parted the Jordan to name some. It all seemed to climax at his showdown with the prophets of Baal and Ashera, the famous contest on Mount Carmel. What is very curious to me however, is that after all of that, when Elijah went into a state of fear, depression and abandonment, God didn't say, "After all I've done for you... this is what you do?" No. Instead, God displayed His presence to Elijah in a gentle whisper.

The heart of the Lord is so pure and true towards those that love Him and want to be close to Him. His heart is to comfort those who mourn, extend the gospel to the poor and bind up the broken. That's His beautiful heart towards you.

We learn from Elijah's plight as he lay in that cave begging God to rescue him, that we are never as alone as we feel. God is always there. Even in a gentle whisper. It may not be a windstorm, an earthquake or a fire, but He is there. A short while after this incident, Elijah received personal transport to heaven in a chariot of fire. There he ascended to meet the one whom his soul loved. Just a short while before, he was begging to die. We are never closer to victory than in our moments of greatest struggle. It's so important to stay in tune to the Holy Spirit.

Elijah was so in tune with God's heart, that when Jesus went up to the mount of transfiguration, Elijah appeared with Moses and they were having a conversation with Jesus. WOW! What a relationship with God... what a miracle. That miracle is available to all of us today.

"Go out and stand before me on the mountain," the LORD told him. And as Elijah stood there, the LORD passed by, and a mighty windstorm hit the mountain. It was such a terrible blast that the rocks were torn loose, but the LORD was not in the wind. After the wind there was an earthquake, but the LORD was not in the earthquake. And after the earthquake there was a fire, but the LORD was not in the fire. And after the fire there was the sound of a gentle whisper. When Elijah heard it, he wrapped his face in his cloak and went out and stood at the entrance of the cave. And a voice said, "What are you doing here, Elijah?" [1 Kings 19:11-13 NLT]

# A HAIRY OBSESSION

This morning I was browsing through the news headlines and the death toll in the war on terrorism is "up"... someone else has lost a son. More suicide bombers are going into eternity and taking innocents with them. What a shame. The late Anna Nicole's corpse is still in the media... being fought over. And then suddenly I was bombarded by a trend. One headline read: Losing hair? How to gain style while going bald! Another: Trump's hair on the line at Wrestle mania! And then the mother lode: Britney Spears shaves her hair... she's bald!

I am not a fan of the bubblegum pop-star's coiffure and certainly not her music but I shudder to think of the numerous young women who have been plunged into the abyss of pubescent confusion. "Wow Britney shaved her head?" I suppose if baldness was inevitable... In fact I have friends that look pretty nice bald.

The problem really isn't in the follicular deprivation of the songstress... but in the moral vacuum that's invading us. If we really look through the eyes of our Savior we would have seen the trouble looming long ago. Children who "make it big" in music and Hollywood... and then all the others who emulate them.

They demonstrate the glitz and the glamour of young minds with the pumped-up, pushed-up, pressed-on, squeezed–in, glued-on, held-up, tucked-in, extended, injected, and tired bodies. Then they're miserable. Checking in and out of rehab and in and out of marriages, divorcing their families and then having children of their own to share in the confusion of living... and who fights for the body of the dead... really?

Oh that we would pray for God to open our eyes to see the truth. That we would not look with envy for what we suppose others may have... for what we have is greater! A treasure in earthen vessels, that is of God and not of us. We would certainly do better to emulate the star... whose body, no one could fight over! Because, by the third day, no grave could hold that body down. Jesus is alive. Copy that! The bible said it best: Proverbs 23:17-18 Don't for a minute envy careless rebels; soak yourself in the Fear of GOD— (The Message)

That's where your future lies. Then you won't be left with an armload of nothing. An armload of nothing... and handfuls of hair. No thanks!

# GOOD HEAVENS! 2019?!

Darth Vader was nothing more than just an alien to me until I met Curt. Then I was properly introduced to the galaxy far, far away and I became a fan... Cyborgs, half human/half machines, AI and robots that take over the world. We've seen the movies. As long as those things are science fiction I am content to watch them over buttered pop-corn. However, this morning, the cyborg reality beamed itself into my human universe and made me wake up.

On Good Morning America, they interviewed the woman who was fitted with the first "real" bionic arm. It's not just an electronic or robotic arm or prosthesis; it is actually connected to and operated by impulses from her brain. She just has to think it and it moves as naturally as any living limb on any human. Except, this arm is bionic: much stronger, more durable... can be tanned by changing the "skin". OK... so you've seen it on TV before. But wait. There were two scientists who have linked their brains together by electrodes and can communicate through their minds... one to the other. They can read each other's thoughts and converse electronically. Wouldn't you say that's a bit Battlestar Galactica-ish?

So what if in four years, robots are marketed that think, behave and even "feel" like humans. Yes "feel". I didn't think it possible either... but we feel because of sensory cells and nerve endings which send impulses to the brain. Scientist can put "sensory cells and nerves" on the surfaces of robots that can send impulses to the brain as well and the brain can be programmed to react in human ways... in every way identical to us. In fact scientists say they can program robots to "progressively" develop and learn, just like a child. They could be "perfect": perfect memories, perfect looks, perfect manners... Robots could easily replace us in every situation of employment... think about it. There was a human-like-robot, of Asian ethnicity, and she looked 100% human. Eyes blinked and skin dimpled when she smiled. You're arguing: "Well they still won't be human and it won't be the same"... and you're right. It won't.

God made a soul and spirit in each one of us. Our bodies are the most insignificant part of who we really are... yet we spend most of our time, energy and resources in making this body look and feel good. Where is the sense in that? Shouldn't we invest in the parts of us that will last forever... an eternity?

If God delays His coming, then those may be the only parts that differentiate man from machine. By the way, there are over 3000 HLL (high level) computer languages. Go figure! Just when I learned Spanish and French!

# I AM 11,584 DAYS OLD TODAY!

Every morning I watch a "happy birthday" segment while I get dressed for work. It's no ordinary birthday wish though. All of the birthday boys and girls are over 100 years old. While listening to the comments made about them, I find a common thread in most, I'd say 19 out of 20 cases. A few common threads actually:

1. They grew up on a farm... and still live on one. Most of them still keep a garden.
2. They all have a hobby.
3. They attribute their longevity to God, faith and church.

I imagine the millions of people who watch morning TV nod their heads in agreement at the first, second and then snicker under "enlightened" breaths at the simple-mindedness of the "old geezer" when they hear the third... then pop some Prozac and join the rat-race. I wonder if the busy business tycoon and skinny-as-a-jerky-strip socialite ever stop to take God's advice and listen to the wisdom of the aged? I wonder if they realize that human life is temporary. And, unlike our elderly friends, it's often cut short before we expect it. 70 years is the average... it's a lifetime but gone before we know it.

What have we done to make those 70 years matter? Have we typed, surfed, filed, counted, saved, collected, and dreamed? Have we lost sleep, skipped holidays, ignored relationships, snubbed God... putting them all on the back burner for a later date? I am 11,584 days old today. 278,028 hours (plus or minus a couple by the time you read this). On this, the 278,028th hour of my existence I will do something that will last an eternity.

"Oh God, my Creator, thank you for my life. Thank you my Savior for giving your life to rescue mine. Thank you Holy Spirit for being my friend every moment since I breathed my first breath." There. That mattered.

Proverbs 3 (NIV)
[1] My son, do not forget my teaching, but keep my commands in your heart,[2] for they will prolong your life many years and bring you prosperity. [3] Let love and faithfulness never leave you; bind them around your neck, write them on your heart.

# TICKLE YOUR OWN ARMPIT!

Ever did something that you knew was a waste of time but you did it anyway? Me? Never... except maybe that one time, and oh yes that other time, and the day after that...

I've never been big on video games... probably because by the time we became addicted to them I had graduated... from college LOL! However, I must make a confession. Circa 2000, while going through a peculiar time in my life, I found an online game that occupied too much of my time and a tiny portion of brain cells. God forbid I reveal the number of unproductive hours surrendered to the ruthless one eyed monster but that game, which is no longer available, certainly made me smile.

It consisted of juxtaposing random words into a certain order and hoping they evolve into a readable sentence. Time runs out and then the 10 or so people you're playing against all vote for the best sentence. I know. The utter frenzy and heart-stopping excitement of wacky sentence formation may seem as foreign as a Bedouin to you... but trust me... it was exciting.

Point is, I squandered a healthy chunk of precious time on something that seemed to profit nothing. I could say that was a mistake... but I prefer to file it under... "Diversion". Just one of the things I did to cheer myself up. Sometimes I think that someone needs to remind me that that's OK. Laugh for no reason, tell yourself a joke, tickle your own armpit and make that mouth curl up and show those pearly whites... it's good medicine. Proverbs 17:22 "A cheerful heart is good medicine, but a crushed spirit dries up the bones." (NIV)

# A SPEEDO AND A GOOD LAUGH

The Olympics were in Sydney in 2000 and I was glued to the TV because Van den Hoogenband and Ian Thorpe would be battling for the gold in the 100m freestyle. But what I was about to see was one  of those images that will last forever in my mind and always make me feel like laughing and crying at the same time. This man from New Guinea was standing alone in the starting blocks. His other two competitors had been disqualified for false starting. He looked a little funny because while other swimmers were decked off in Fat Skin body suits, he was wearing "briefs" made from terrycloth with a drawstring. Tears of pity welled up in my eyes.

His name is Eric Moussambani and this was the first time he would be swimming the 100m in his life.

In fact he had never even seen a 50m pool before that week in Sydney. He was a "goodwill wildcard" contestant. The Olympic committee picked a random swimmer to compete in order to encourage other countries to participate. They picked Eric.

The signal sounded and Eric blew my mind. He didn't slice into the water with the svelte of a trained streamlined athlete, no. He flopped his entire body into the water and began huffing and puffing his way across the pool. My jaw dropped open and I stared in disbelief at his flailing arms and the gigantic splashes of water all around him as he beat the water to death, splashing loudly and slowly across.

My tears of pity turned into I'm laughing-so-hard-I'm-crying tears, and it was almost painful. I laughed so much I couldn't even call anyone to watch with me. 50m was over and he turned and started swimming back. My laughter turned into anxiety. This poor fellow was taking in water. If I wasn't comforted by the fact that he was surrounded by the world's best swimmers who could jump in and save him at any time, I would have called 911 myself. I watched through the parted fingers of my hands which were firmly planted over my eyes. This man looked like he was drowning. His hands went everywhere and so did the water. Those last 15m were torture to him... AND to me. In the painful last seconds he made one noble lurch at the pool's edge, touched the finishing line and hung on to the side for dear life. He was coughing, gasping, shaking and in shock. But something had changed in the stadium. Every person in the stadium was on their feet screaming and cheering for Moussambani. He had the worst qualifying time ever in that race. In fact he was slower than the qualifying time for the 200m. In fact, the computers were not equipped to register his time... the numbers didn't go that high. But he finished. The race is still not for the swift, but for those who can finish! By the way, after that race, Speedo outfitted him in a brand new streamlined wetsuit. He loved it.

# THE THING ABOUT BEING TRINI...

The thing about being Trini is that it springs up on you... out of nowhere. After living in a foreign country for almost two decades, the culture, twang and mannerisms of the native people are bound to creep up and set in, but all of a sudden *BAM* the Trini in me wakes up. Just so. One day you're just moving along and you hear a Soca beat and it's like you're there, eating curry chicken and roti on Maracas Beach... listening to the breaking waves and watching your little brother get tumbled in the water like a cat in a dryer.

Another time, you're minding your own business and somebody cracks a joke that a Trini would call stale and suddenly you're at Chin's Parlour sucking down a flav-o-rite milky before your mother catches you spending the change. East Indians can tell you're not from India; Hispanics know you're not Hispanic and unless people know another Trini... you hear the question, "Where are you from?" And just like a standard 1 poem, recited directly from TV when all we had was TTT channels 2 & 13 you say with pride, "Trinidad and Tobago, the most southerly isle of the Caribbean," and sometimes, if the listener is interested you add, "land of the Scarlet Ibis, home of the steel pan, calypso and limbo."

And then *BAM* you're there again. Lining up, toe-to-the-line for morning worship in primary school, smelling like coconut oil because your mother said it was nice. Liming at Gulf city, taking a maxi taxi, eating doubles, preserve mango and drinking Apple J. Thing about being Trini is the realization that God is nice. Real nice. To take my ancestors from far away and drop them on an island, so that many years later I would have a heritage that is as rich, free and wonderful as the one I have now!

Today be grateful for where you are and where God has brought you from. I am.

# IT WAS THE FUNNIEST THING...

Groan... ouch, limp, limp... that was the state of most of the dancers on Monday. We had dance practice on Sunday, so after back bends, stretching and 2 hours of dance, by Monday the pain had gotten the best of them. I laughed, not at them but with them... OK so maybe a little AT them. Thing is though, the ones who were unaccustomed to stretching their muscles and strength, were the ones who hurt the most. Doing things we're unaccustomed to always causes a little discomfort. But like exercise, it makes us stronger, more flexible and better at what we're trying to do.

I remember the first time I climbed to the top of the telephone pole at youth camp and tried to stand on it with both feet. The wind shaking the pole was nothing compared to my shaking legs. I distinctly remember thinking how funny it was that even though I willed my legs to be still they vibrated like they were hooked to a 2 ton jackhammer. All the while I'm screaming in fear, trying to be funny and make myself laugh, singing "Jesus take the wheel" at the top of my lungs. I closed my eyes and lunged off the pole. Seconds later I was hanging from a trapeze by my hands, I had done it!

The road behind Jesus, since I am a follower, is a demanding one. Not very wide and easy. It's challenging, treacherous and often stretches me beyond comfortable. But every time I take that challenge, speak despite the fear, act despite the jeers, stand up for WHO I believe in, I'm being sculpted into the lean, undefeatable awesomeness of my Savior.

Dance practice may hurt, but it makes a beautiful dancer. Being a disciple may be tough, but it's worth it to look like my Lord!

2 Cor 3:18 "And we all, who with unveiled faces contemplate the Lord's glory, are being transformed into his image with ever-increasing glory, which comes from the Lord, who is the Spirit." (NIV)

# I FOUND A LETTER

When I look back to the major catalysts in my life, they were all fueled by something I had written on paper. When I broke up with my first boyfriend, it was because my father had found a letter he wrote... trouble. When I lost my first long-term job, it was because another employee had found a poem I had written about the perils and burdens I experienced at that job and felt compelled to show it to the owner... more trouble. I even got in "trouble" once, at university because a poem I wrote accidentally got handed-in between papers in a thesis. The lecturer thought I had a crush on him... eeww.

But writing helps me organize my thoughts and clarify my misconceptions and opinions. It's the first step toward making my wistful imagination a reality and God knows it's the only thing that keeps me from forgetting everything when I'm doing too many things at once. I have a book... well I actually have two. They're not journals; they're quick-thought books. To write those musings that arises at the most unpredictable times. You know- the things you can never remember later.

Writing has gotten me in trouble, but it has also gotten me closer to my visions. I communicate with my Father that way, most honestly I think, because my heart AND my mind is focused on Him. I am a firm advocate of "writing my vision boldly and clearly." Yesterday I found a letter I had written to Curtis 11 years ago. It was written over a period of 3 months and it took me back to those days like no treasured memory stored in my mind can. I wrote, "If 10 years from now, we take each other for granted, I hope someone will remind us of today, these times, when we fight for minutes together."

Well someone did. Yesterday, I was glad I had written that letter, because I vividly remembered how much we really did fight for minutes together, realized how much I take him for granted and completely understood the miracle that God worked in me, by the words I wrote. God's own word works miracles every day, since the day He breathed it. His word became flesh, in the person of His Son and we looked upon the Glory of God... amazing. Don't forget to go back today and read those words He wrote to you so many years ago, words that are fully alive and changing lives every day.

Update: It has now been 20 years since I wrote that letter and I grieve because I no longer have it. It was lost along with all my other letters in Hurricane Sandy... but I read it enough times that I know most of it by heart.

Like God's word.   What a beautiful situation: words that are written on our hearts so that no one could ever take them away.

# VIRGINIA TECH SHOOTING

By now, you've heard the news. More than 30 people breathed their last breath when a student opened fire on the Virginia Tech campus. It was the topic of every news station, the subject of every blog and on the minds and hearts of everyone who has heard about it. It can never really be significant enough and you can never feel it in its severity unless it's your brother, sister, son or daughter lying face down in their own blood, or unless you are the one staring point blank into the barrel of a madman's 9mm.

Oh God have mercy on us. America is crying out as numerous people, parents, siblings, spouses, friends and children grieve. Unanswered questions fly up to God, some from lips that have not turned His way in many years, others from those He hears from every day. Would knowing the reasons alleviate the pain? No. I don't know the reasons. I cannot answer "why". Not at all. I know this though: Each day I'm sure I forget something… certainly. But each day I also remember something… certainly: I remember to pray… to call out to my God and Father, on behalf of my family and loved ones, for mercy. Because there is no telling what my next breath will bring my way, but there is peace knowing that He is in charge of that next breath… and everyone that follows. No man, on this earth, can take that away, unless He says so.

Today I pray for rest for all who grieve and for God to give His angels charge over you, my friend, to keep you from accident, harm, danger, seen and unseen. In the name of His son Jesus.

# SEND ME

Send me to the places where people need you most
Where they're thirsting for the water of Life
Flowing freely from the throne
Of God
My master

Lead me to a valley where the hills loom large around
And the only source of refuge is a
Bubbling from the ground
O Spring
My water

Show me countless faces longing deeply for a light
Where a vision may have perished, send a
Glimmer in the night
The Word
My Savior

Make me a useful vessel on this broken, dying sphere

Speed my steps, fill me up
Let me take you there
True Hope
My Father

Write me upon your hands and heart, let me never stray
To heed the calls of transience
Or wander from the way
Of Truth
My Lord

Send me to the places where people need you most
To pour the flood of endless life
To quench each thirsting soul
O God!
Send me.

# A MISSIONARY SONG

They that wait, once thought
That God was not around
That days and nights, account for life
Go get a job, become a wife
Belong. Accept. Conform.

They that wait, once pondered
If what they felt was true
Still then a child, still free and wild
Causing panic, was she beguiled
Obey. Inquire. Pursue.

They that wait, discovered
A wealth that few will see
To hear the call, devote their all
Fight in battle, stand up tall
Believe. Commit. Agree.

They that wait, believed
With all their heart that soon

The earth would shake, it's time forsake
That men would faint for Heaven's sake
Reveal. Amaze. Consume.

They that wait, once waited
And waiting was no more
For they grew wings, did splendid things
Rose high above as Priests and Kings
Increase. Ascend. Soar!

# I NEED A RUNNING PARTNER!

Until a few years ago, no one in my family, as far as I knew has ever had cancer. I pray no one ever will. My husband's father died from leukemia when Curt was just 9... so they felt the sting of that bitter enemy. 1 in 3 people will be diagnosed with cancer sometime in their lives. 1 in 3. God help us.

So we pray for our parents, sisters, brothers, children, friends. We pray that God, our healer will continue to spare our lives and give us good health, confident in His ability to keep us. AND... we pray for those who are already fighting the battle for their health, confident in hope that they will overcome.

One year I decided that I was going to run in the Sprint for Life 5K Run & Walk. I needed someone to train with. I had a lot of work before I could coax my legs into moving constantly for 5K.

I thought about how hard it would be to get my

body to do something as simple as a 5K. I know that it's nothing compared to chemo, to wondering if today is the day you have to say goodbye to your family or to the physical and emotional torture that that disease can be.

I wanted to run to help. I offered my faith and my works and set out to seek a friend to do something with me that God willing may not directly benefit us, but will help someone else.

And then last year I watched God heal one of my spiritual sons from cancer. In the doctor's words, "it looked like it was rooted out." And this morning, I offer for you and your loved ones a prayer of healing. That our Father, Jehovah Rophe, will speak healing to your bodies and hearts.

# IS IT SHAMU?

I was on my way to San Antonio, to SeaWorld and the riverwalk. I was excited. We were about 155 miles outside of San Antonio and we were steadily driving through a thick Houston fog, listening to some music on the CD player.

I must confess, I'm a first time kind of individual. The first time I went to SeaWorld I cried. Don't be embarrassed for me... I'm alright with it. The first time I saw a beluga whale swim past me at Sea World tears just poured down my face. Granted, I must have been a strange sight. I was about 26 years old.

I remember being totally overwhelmed by how magnificent they were but MORE overwhelmed by the INCREDIBLE GOD who took the time to design them so perfectly. That's exactly what I was thinking.

I've cried at other strange times too, at Disney

World when Fantasia took my breath away, at a dance recital when the dancers were in perfect synch and totally immersed in their movements and at the theater when the Phantom hit the high note.

Creativity is obviously my passion. Expressed in the arts, it's one of my favorite ways to worship. A wise man once told me; "use your passion for God. I'll tell you how to find out what your passion is. It's that thing which makes you laugh out loud, makes your heart tremble with anticipation and your jaw clench with excitement, it makes you cry for joy... even against your better judgment."

So I'm off to SeaWorld and even though it's doubtful that I'll cry again, I am still certain I'll be in awe of my creator.

Man's creativity is a drop in an endless ocean compared to God's, I said to myself as I looked at the yellow port-a-potty we just passed in the middle of the freeway. Hmmm... God wins.

Praise be to Almighty God, creator of the Universe and all that is in it.

## MY SOUL FOR A KLONDIKE?

Golden vanilla ice cream covered with a smooth chocolate shell... on a stick. It wasn't a real Klondike bar. In Trinidad, it was "dark and gold"; and when every other ice cream was 75 cents, a dark and gold was $3.50.

I couldn't get one. I only had $1 a day and after my snack at recess... I couldn't save up enough. So... one day I did the unthinkable. Even though I couldn't afford it, every lunch time I'd venture across the street to the shop (in Trinidad kids could do this) and look down into the freezer. There they all were. All lined up and I could smell them.

That fateful Friday I stared down into the freezer at the ice cream and a gleam caught my eye. There, on the floor, was a miracle. 25 cent pieces. Many. Shinning.

I looked around quickly to see if the owner of this

treasure was in the vicinity and I saw no one. I bent down and scooped them up to take them to the store owner and on the way up from a crouch, I saw the ice cream.

My 7 years of Christian upbringing kicked in and I marched over to the cashier and handed over the loot. Then I received an ice-cream as a reward!

Actually... this would have been an ideal ending but not quite what occurred. Instead, Sharo carefully counted 14 coins and deftly let the others sail to the floor like dying leaves on an autumn oak. I reached into the freezer and wrapped shaking fingers around the icy-cold temptation. I paid. I exited. I ran. I stood outside the store, heart beating furiously, opened the wrapper and bit in.

I looked up at my school and noticed that the yard looked rather deserted. Lunch time was over and all the children were back in class. I had spent the better part of the hour standing there outside the freezer, fighting a war in my mind. A war my spirit lost.

Frantically, I looked for a trash can and tossed the stolen bar, wrapper and everything, and madly dashed across the street and back to class. All I could tell my curious teacher was..."ice-cream... didn't see". He let it slide. I was right. "Ice-cream... didn't see" was enough to rid me of a one time tragedy.

This story is not about stealing. It's about the mind and the temptations we face every day, at every age. It's about the repercussions of sin and blindness... because that thing we want is what we think will make us happy. WRONG. I spent many years paying back that $3.50. I gave many allowances away, not in order to win God's forgiveness... but to win my own. I did.

Note to self: Guilt is the worst flavor on any dessert.

# WAITING TO EXHALE

I know there is a movie somewhere by that name... didn't see it. But... I know what it feels like.

Just for experience sake, I just held my breath as long as I could. 55 seconds. I think I could go longer, if I did it a few times. The first few seconds are bearable... but it's those last 10 or so... when your brain starts feeling like its pushing against the walls of your skull and your lungs feel like they're filling up with oil, it's those seconds that are the hardest.

That's how I feel when I'm waiting for a GOD ANSWER. You know, those tough decisions that you couldn't possibly make without Him. It feels like I'm holding my breath. Exhaling is my greatest wish and only when He says "Yes" or "No", only then it feels like I can.

I feel like that today. But don't feel bad for me. I'm excited. I know whatever answer He gives me, will be the RIGHT one. I'm certain and thankful that it's up to Him and my decisions will be perfect... because they will be HIS. What an excellent hope and blessed assurance.

No wonder I love Him so.

His word says He will give me the desires of my heart. When this revelation finally got in my spirit, I held tightly to it. He won't give me what I think my heart desires... instead, He will give my heart the desires it should have. My heart's desires were put there by Him... and they shall surely come to pass.

Why not let Him give you the desires of your heart.

# OUR POISONED PUPPY

I'm sad because one night someone poisoned my brother's dog. My father said it must be the man who sneaks in at night to steal the mangoes off the trees in their yard. The dog was an excellent watch dog. He would bark up a storm. The vet said that someone must have soaked a piece of meat in poison and fed it to him.

Jason was very upset. When he took the doggy to the vet, it was still alive but gasping for air and not doing very well. The sorrow I felt is nothing compared to what my brother Jason must have felt. That was his dog. Just imagine how God's heart breaks when He sees us being poisoned by the enemy. Sin is only pleasant for a short time. He longs for us to be safe, whole and fed only the truth of His word.

Sometimes the danger that we encounter comes disguised as pleasure. Today let us be watchful, vigilant, and knowing that we have an adversary. But let us also rejoice that when we feed at the Master's table, we are safe.

# AN EXERCISE IN FUTILITY

It's like trying to stop the neighbor's cats from pooping in my flower beds. I chased them off and sprayed them with water, dotted the flower scape with so many moth balls, it looked like there was a war between two armies of snowmen, in which they were all decapitated.

The cats still came. After a while there was no dirt left in the flower beds to cover up the piles of poop because all the dirt was already covering piles of poop. So the cats won. We paved over our flower beds with cement. Now you can walk to my front door and not hold your breath.

Sometimes to solve a problem, drastic measures have to be taken. We can't go on trying to "cover up" mistakes and wrongs in our lives forever. We need to deal with the problem at its root... at least as close to the root as we can get. You see, I may not be able to assassinate the cats, just like I cannot "kill" the devil, but I can eliminate the part of me that invites him to attack. I will not put myself in a compromising position.

Well last week I planted another flower bed, not in the same place though. Farther away... and so far it's been poop free. My friend said cayenne pepper will keep them away. So I got some. We'll see!

# SOUP FOR BRAINS

 Mythbusters is a show about 2 weird guys who try to disprove myths and blow up toilets and other household appliances. I've seen it a few times, and decided that it's way more intellectually stimulating to believe that an umbrella CAN be converted into a weapon that doesn't include old ladies whacking a handicapped robber over the head with one.

Theories, assumptions, hypothesis, guesses... life is made up of so many of them and sometimes I think they're all floating around like balloons in my head. You know, those times when you can't seem to concentrate on one thought before the next one bullies it out of the way and plops itself on to your brain couch?

Too many things to think about. I need, I perceive, a cerebral Mythbuster to pop the air from those floating balloons, and un-crowd my mind. Wait a sweet second! I have one of those.

- *POP* there goes the thoughts of "where will I be living in 12 months"
- *POP* goes "will these people recall anything I've said"
- *POP* goes "I wonder if he's upset or she's upset with me again"
- *POP* goes "I wonder what they're saying about me now"
- *POP* goes "so does money matter or not? pick one"

The Holy Spirit is the MASTER MYTHBUSTER... telling me that "everything will work out for my benefit, because I'm in love with the Almighty God." He occupies the center seat on my brain couch and life becomes simpler again.

I couldn't live without HIM. Mythbusters even did an episode on the possibility of death by noxious gases caused by flatulence. They proved it couldn't happen. They obviously don't know some of the people I've met. LOL

# MY 33<sup>RD</sup> BIRTHDAY!

Today my MySpace changed itself... the age part on the profile changed from 32 to 33 while I wasn't looking. It didn't surprise me, but it did make me laugh!

Today marks 33 years since the day tears streamed down my 17 year old mother's cheeks as she cried in pain to bring me into this world. It's the best day of my life. I've never lived this long, never breathed so much air and never has my heart clocked more beats in time than this very day!

I have lived to see the earth dance around the sun in honor of the Father's will 33 times! I have never known my friends, cared for my family, lived my life or loved my husband longer than this very day... I'm loving it.

This is the best day of the best year of my life so far. I can't wait to see what happens next.

Curt left my present on the bed this morning and left for work. I was so tired; I didn't even hear him leave (my ear plugs probably helped). A few minutes later, I managed to force my eyes open and caught a glimpse of a red, yellow, green and blue gift bag! Still asleep I stuck my hand into the bag and pulled out a box. Wow! My eyes flew open and all sleep vanished, evaporated and disintegrated in a second! I've been fully awake since!

Thank God for this day... the best day of my life... so far.

# BEFORE I SAW EVAN ALMIGHTY

I've seen the previews and the movie looks funny. The weirdo with the beardo. I'm going to see the movie when it comes out.

Really though, even before this movie, the story of Noah is hilarious! Old guy, building a giant boat, miles away from the sea, for decades, muttering something about "rain", which according to the bible, no one had seen at that time. Talk about stick-to-it-ive-ness!

I almost have to beat myself over the head to make myself floss my own teeth every day. Even though I know it's the right thing to do. Don't even talk about exercise! How many of those plans have I stuck to? Not too many.

You know, what if, on the 89th or 100th day of the 60th year... Noah gave up "That's it! I'm fed up of people making fun of me. My hands are tired and

there is NO water falling from the sky! I QUIT!"
Then the flood would have come just as God said,
and the human race and every animal on earth would
be extinct.　God knew exactly who to choose!
Someone who would hear God's instructions and
follow them... no matter what.　God give me courage,
determination, persistence and perseverance like
Noah, to fulfill the calling that you have given me...
no matter what.　I'm ready for it... just as long as I
don't start growing excessive gobs of facial hair!!

# BIRD DANCE

They circled like vultures, around and around, past my house and down the street. They slowed down to a crawl, scoping out the front yard, studying, taking mental notes and as soon as they passed my driveway they sped off again. I watched them do this at least 5 times... they didn't stop. Each time I watched them pass, I wondered. Then I would shake myself out of my thoughts and get back to the woman asking me the price of the already assembled puzzle, with two pieces dislodged. That was a Saturday and it was my yard sale.

Since we're putting our house up for sale, we're trying to sell off as much unnecessary baggage as possible. Between hot beads of sweat on my brow, quasi-dehydration, tons of sale items and my ever-effervescent 1 year old niece... I had my hands full. But I still found the moments to wonder about the strange people that kept passing my house, slowing down... doing their weird auto bird dance. No dead carcass here.

In the afternoon, I closed the sale and packed all the remaining stuff in boxes. I left it at the front of the house and called the neighborhood charity store to come for a pick up and went inside. I had a shower, put my niece to nap and stepped outside and great-gobs-of-steaming-revelation... there they were! The bird people. They were going through the stuff in the boxes... taking it. Eyes wide open, mouth ajar and almost amazed... I realized. They were just circling so that they could get for free what they didn't think was worth paying a penny for. Oh the agony.

So, I see there are things that are valuable to us, such as our standards, integrity, dreams, convictions, purity in thought and actions and many of us willingly give those away for little. But the enemy will wait till we put those things on display. Wait for the moment when we let our guard down and do not watch diligently after them and he swoops in for the kill. He takes it for free. The devil came to steal, kill and destroy. I'm not at all mad at the people. I am glad and hope the things they got meet their needs.

However, today I'm thinking more clearly about what God meant when He said to "WATCH and pray" because the devil is like a lion, looking for someone to kill. Keep a close eye on the things that endear you to our Lord, His kingdom and His cross... they are way more precious than gold.

# I CAN'T LIVE WITHOUT YOU

The TRINITY: God in 3 persons explained fully so ANYONE can understand. Wouldn't that be great?

A pastor said one Sunday morning, "If Jesus walked into the church, what would you do" and all the while I was thinking, "He did" walk in. All day Friday and Saturday, that was the gist of the conversation the Holy Spirit and I were having. This pastor had a similar conversation it seemed.

The Holy Spirit gets the short end of the stick from us. BIG MISTAKE on our part. The Holy Spirit is as much God as Jehovah and Jesus Christ. As Christ was ALL God in the Flesh, the Holy Spirit is ALL God in Spirit. I think we miss that. Totally.

The Holy Spirit is the person of the Trinity, GOD that chooses to stay with us constantly while we live on this earth. We say, "If Jesus were standing in front of me, I'd eat dirt. Just bow down and fall at His feet!" WHY? Because He is God. Well... GOD IS HERE... the Holy Spirit. Why aren't we face first on the dirt, worshipping? He's here. God with us. Keeping us in God until Christ returns! He didn't have to come. God could have abandoned us and said, "fend for yourself till the rapture... I already died for you... see if you can make it" But He didn't. He chose to come in Spirit constantly checking us to keep us ready for heaven, because we slip so easily. He WANTS us to make heaven. God made it EASY, very EASY if we listen, because He came Himself to give us guidance step by step and still we wander in ignorance... ignoring His voice. No wonder Jesus said that whoever blasphemed the Holy Spirit would not forgiven. NO wonder. Because God is still with us... in the Form of the Holy Spirit and as we have done since time began we shut out the voice of God.

Recognize the voice of God. Who HE IS... God the father, God the Son and God the Holy Spirit... and worship Him. Thank you Holy Spirit, God with me... every day.

I can't live without you.

# BOOTY GLOW

 Whoosh... there it goes... Ever went butterfly or firefly catching? Even though it hasn't been a recent outing for me, as a child I loved chasing after the illusive insects. Trouble is though, once I had them in my hands, or in the jar, they never seemed quite as magnificent or mysterious as they were in flight.

Scientists and evolutionists try to convince me that fireflies "evolved" into creatures that developed a butt full of LUCIFERASE AND LUCIFERIN genetically combined to make them luminescent. The glow is a mating ritual and defense mechanism. Apparently, according to evolution, only fireflies and glow worms were smart enough to decipher the genetic code that makes their booties glow. Too bad for the lady bugs, moths, and cockroaches and other less evolved species that have regular bug behinds. Strange, even though they face the same predators and live in the same environments... yeah... hmm. Point is... God made them. He designed them and in His peculiar and amazing care and creativity, made a bug that twinkles. Sure, it's a mating signal (it's natural to use your best feature to attract a mate), sure it's a defense mechanism (a light in me scares away predators all the time), but it's a tiny light demonstrating the loving nature of a Great BIG GOD.

# BREAKFAST AT LA MADELINE

I had breakfast at La Madeline and an epiphany. Standing in line for a macchiato, the quaint ambiance and the smell of coffee stirred me like frothy milk foam on the top of my highly anticipated steaming cup.

CAN YOU REALLY RECOGNIZE GOD'S VOICE WHEN HE SPEAKS TO YOU? Are you sure it's Him? Many of you have said you are not sure you heard from Him. You're almost certain. I want to show you how to be sure. No fancy hermeneutics, exegesis and theological explanations. Just plain simple, practical truth... in English!

Refreshing. That's what I'm writing about next. If I had to put a disclaimer for this new phase of my life, I'd say: I know this entry will bless some, offend others, encourage some, incite others, tickle some and disgust others... but the thoughts expressed are my heart. Inspired by my love for my Savior and you, my friend. So, don't ask me to change it, because I won't anymore. I won't be afraid to speak, because those who would shut me up are no match for what is embedded deeply within me - Christ's anointing, no less! Christ's anointing teaches me the truth on everything I need to know about myself and Him, uncontaminated by a single lie. I will live deeply in what I was taught (1John 2:27).

Every day we live in Christ we become a little more like Him. Then one day, we will see Him, as He is, and we shall be like Him. As I sipped my coffee I realized that the voice of Him who loves me is precious to my soul. I know His voice. I recognize the way He speaks to me. It is His will that those who follow Him... hear Him.

# CALL OFF THE GUARDS

Call off the guards, she's not insane... she's not trying to attack the queen; she's just running around with hands waving because she's excited, a little bit anxious and a whole lot of bug-eyed-amazed. That's me. That's where I am right now. I've been leaving for a while... but this time... I'm leaving for New York in August. How do we move to a city and start a life in a strange place, just because God said to? Just like Abraham did it by way of Haran.

How do we lead God's people to a land of promise that we too must believe by faith? Moses did it by way of the wilderness.

How do we give up the comfort of home to preach to a city we do not know and people we've never seen? Jonah did it by way of a really big fish.

Spare us the fish Oh Lord! I am excited to start Hope in NYC. Psyched about In This Life Inc. All the while knowing that if GOD doesn't do it, it won't get done. All my life I've said, "I'll go Lord, send me" and now as He sends me I know with all my heart, that I won't go if He doesn't go, and wherever He goes, I will follow. Meanwhile, as I run around with flailing arms, I will try not to bump in to Curt or Jodi.

(Jodi is my friend who moved to New York with us in obedience to the Holy Spirit. She has been a part of HopeNYC church since day 1.)

# BLINDNESS... THE MOVIE... THE PROBLEM

"The only thing more terrifying than blindness is being the only one who can see" says Julianne Moore's character in the movie. It's based on the premise that everyone else has contracted a mysterious disease and has gone blind. Utter chaos erupts as vehicles crash as motorists go blind, airplanes fall out of the sky and adults and children alike are plunged into the terrifying unknown. Scary.

Even more terrifying is that in the spiritual realm (which exists regardless of our belief in or lack thereof) it looks a lot like this. Jesus said, we have eyes but we do not see. We grope about life, stuck in routines, looking like we know exactly what we're doing, because we've done it so many times before.

Knowing how is so far removed from knowing why. There is a difference though: spiritual blindness is a choice. He said it perfectly: "You say, 'I am rich; I have acquired wealth and do not need a thing." But you do not realize that you are wretched, pitiful, poor, blind and naked. Tell me if that sounds anything like our world. We want to exclude ourselves from the "blind ones" and assume that Jesus was talking about those who do not follow Him. No He wasn't... not really... not at all. Jesus was actually talking to casual "Christians." We who are "neither hot nor cold." (Check it out in Rev 3:16-17)

But He is always faithful: there is a cure. He said we could come freely, and He would anoint our eyes so that we could see. Now there's an illuminating experience. To see, like Paul did on the Damascus road, is to come face to face with the Living GOD. You will see the truth, the way and the Life and be irrevocably and utterly changed. Pray that your eyes will be opened.

# TRUE FRIENDSHIPS

"The friendship that can cease has never been real." - Saint Jerome. Philosophers like Aristotle and Cicero had a different take on friendship than most of us do in this 21st century. While we insist that friendships are great "in-spite of" our differences, personalities, moral divides and such, these men attested that it is necessary for souls to be unified, in convictions, perceptions and virtue for true friendship to exist.

While in my life I have regrets... yes, I said it... there are certainly things I would do differently, I have not yet regretted a friendship. There are some that I have lost but I consider them simply hibernating. For the record, I disagree with the philosophers because our Lord went willingly to a cross of pain and shame for "His friends." His friends would be the same ones who held no regard for His deity, who could not equal nor understand His standards of morality, the same ones who rested on

His chest one day and deserted Him the next. Those were the friends for whom He gave His life. He's my friend.

# HERE'S A RIDDLE

What do you call a decade's worth of change?
Answer: The Last 12 months

That's what it's felt like. Today as I pressed through the blustery wind, beating snow and sub zero temperatures, I thought about how much life has changed for me in the past few months. It's almost as dizzying as the swirling white flakes dancing around my bubble jacket. Trudging through the icy sludge, shielding my face from the icy blast and walking as fast as snow boots will allow... I smile. Amidst ALL the changes... He remains the same... evermore FAITHFUL.

On this last fleeting day of a year that has come and gone, I say "thank you" from the deepest part of my soul. Thank you to my amazing and beyond describable Father God... who is the one constant in my frantic life. Time with Him is a moment's rest, a breath of complete peace and a deep sigh of utter relief. It is a safe place, a warm and comfortable home away from the cold and unmerciful outside. To all my family and friends, sent by my Father to add joy to this journey... I wish you the best of blessings today.

I pray today that God pleasantly surprises you around every corner, that He affords you a greater revelation of Himself than ever before and that your joy is increased to fullness. Have a great one in Jesus name.

# BUZZZ BUZZZ

It's 5:30am on Saturday morning, and I'm wishing I had some coffee. Sure, the kitchen is 10 steps away from where I'm sitting with my computer... and the coffee certainly won't make itself, but I don't feel like going. I can almost smell the fresh brewed scent and see the stream of smoke wafting from the warm cup... but it's hardly enough to get me on my feet and propel me into action. I am acutely aware that the caffeine will pop my senses open and even my eyes. My awakening, albeit artificially, might make this 20 degree morning feel like more of a Saturday than it does.

Seems like a tall order for a cup a' joe. I'll get the coffee when I'm good and ready. If my procrastination lends itself to something so trivial, why does it then baffle me when people fail to grasp that making the journey with Christ is a wake up... that does not fade away? It's the open eyes, acute senses and full assurance in a secured future, which is precluded by a decision. Believe. Sometimes it is the perceived loss incurred. You know, loss of familiarity, like this couch I'm sitting on... maybe it's a mess of other things. One thing's for sure though... life in Christ is not "like a box of chocolates." I know what I get: "they that wait on the Lord, will have their strength renewed. They will soar on wings like eagles; they will run and not grow weary, they will walk and not be faint." I get that. I believe. There's a cup of coffee somewhere calling my name... and it's going to take me getting up off my behind, walking to the kitchen and putting my faith into action.

# DARTS SCHMARTS

There are two ways that I can do this... so I chose. I can contemplate about how much sleep I didn't get, or I can get happy about the time I had to close my eyes in rest. I can lament having to work again... or I can get happy that I have a job and I'm physically and mentally able to perform. You get the idea.

I chose to remember that today is no ordinary day. It is the day that my Lord has made and ordained a blessing in it for me! I chose to live it fully alive and aware of the hand of God. Don't presume that this is an easy task. The choosing is the easy part. Then you get on the train and face the DARTS of life, toil and negativity. Little darts that sting or hurt and one is bearable... but enough, feels fatal. But "fear not"! I hear my Lord say, "For no weapon that is formed against you will prosper." Darts Schmarts.

No dart can penetrate the armor, the shield of faith that is ever before me. The breastplate of righteousness that guards my heart and character, the helmet of salvation, which keeps my mind focused and my will strong, the truth of His word around my waist and my feet ever ready, wearing the message of peace, of my Savior who gave His life a ransom for mine. I go out today strong and un-intimidated, holding fast to His Spirit, His word, my sword with which I can fight every foe. After all, I know how this battle ends, I read the book. May you be blessed today, in His name and may you walk fully alive in the knowledge that He walks with you.

# THE WAITING GAME

Ever ordered anything online? It's like an adventure I think. First you search out the treasure, then you take a deep breath and press enter. You submit your credit card information to someone you've never seen, you add a little extra for processing and shipping and then you wait. Sometimes, you wait some more. Curtis ordered a book online, a neuroscience book for school and he waited. And waited. And you guessed it, the book never came. So he got on the phone and dialed some numbers, spoke with someone, then argued with someone else. He never got His book.

Sometimes I think waiting is my least favorite thing in the world. I'd rather clean my whole house AND yours... twice, than wait. When we submit our request to the Father, often it involves some waiting. Meanwhile if you're like me, you squirm and wiggle and get so ready for it to happen now that you're ready to puke. I feel like I need a seat belt. You learn the hard way that checking the mail box six times a day doesn't make it happen any faster, checking your voicemail or e-mail every 30 seconds doesn't help either. Waiting is a process and there is a trick to easing the pain: DO something! Occupy! Get busy. Waiting is not the same as sitting on our derriere gathering dust. Waiting is a pain but a bearable one when you are certain to get what you're waiting for and what's coming is worth the wait.

Waiting on God to come to your rescue is never blind hope, it's a blessed assurance, that "He will finish the good work that He has already begun in you". He will do exactly what His word says. He will, guaranteed. He delivers, and He's ALWAYS right on time! Every time. As for cleaning your house... some other time... maybe!

# NO THANKS... I'LL HAVE A MUFFIN
## INSTEAD

This morning, (which is a Friday! whoopee!) I read the most disturbing thing. I like the parts in the bible where it talks about the miracles Jesus performed, the importance of love and obedience, the prophets, the poetry, the letters, the wisdom, the law, gospels... I like it all. Tucked between all the "good" stuff though, are some things that automatically engage my gag reflex. You know what I mean, like when you were a kid and your mother hid vegetables in your favorite dessert. Yuck!

This morning in Isaiah, I read something just like that. It started off wonderfully, "How gracious He will be when you cry for help! As soon as He hears, He will answer you. "Yes! Amen!" I was mentally soaring by now and then came the hidden broccoli: "Although the Lord gives you the bread of adversity and the water of affliction." WHAT? That part made my stomach do a somersault. We've all been there, in fact, some of us ARE there. We need God to make a way; we are desperate for His intervention. Sounds like prison food, bread of adversity and the water of affliction. Of all the things I've ever tasted I think those two would have to be the worst. Honestly, after we've been eating and drinking this for a while, we just want to say, "No thanks God, I'll have a muffin instead!" and see if that works! But just before it got the best of me I did the smart thing, and read on! He said, "Whether you turn to the right or to the left, your ears will hear a voice behind you, saying, This is the way; walk in it."

What a promise! Even though things may be rough, He's there my friend, guiding you every step of the way. The night may be long, but your steps are ordered and sure, weeping may endure for the night but joy comes in the morning! Hold on, secure in the knowledge that He who keeps you, doesn't sleep. Even though the process of this bread and water is unpleasant, like the hidden veggies, they make us stronger. Sure they taste like dirt, especially when we love the sweets, but they build us up. And bread and water won't stay in your system forever! So Hold on! It's coming out!

# DO YOU REMEMBER?

You know the first guy to climb Mount Everest? Well, if your name is Marlo Ramdial then you know this like the back of your hand. At his age, mid-fifties, my father has the enviable ability to recall thousands of pieces of trivia and facts that he learned as a child. He can quote hundreds of verses of prose and poetry, random and astonishing historical data and of course, most of the bible... verbatim.

It is a skill I envy. Sometimes I think I do well to remember to put the same color socks on or remember what I had for breakfast. But remembering is sometimes the best thing we can do, especially on a Monday morning when it's hard to get out of bed and even harder to step outside into a 23 degree chill.

Today I smile because I can remember. I remember that my steps are ordered by God, I remember His mercies are new every morning and He has kept His promise to never leave me nor forsake me. I remember that though there are many that venture out alone today, I go with the Spirit of the Almighty on my side and an innumerable cloud of witnesses! I remember His goodness towards me in times past and all the times when I felt there was no way out, and He made a way. I remember that He said to "Put me in remembrance." And I do.

History records that in 1953 Sir Edmund Percival Hillary and his companion, Tensing Norga conquered Mt. Everest. For the final 300 yards they ascended at a blinding speed of 2 to 3 painful steps per minute. They did it slowly, but no one remembers that. All we remember is that they did it... first. Take a moment to remember the good that God has blessed you with. One small step at a time, you overcome that anything that stands in your way.

# 2 DOLLAR BILLS

Somebody once said that, the best way to stay happy is to remember the things that made you sad, depressed, angry or upset and don't do them again! I know. Deep.

One day as I dashed out of one train and was headed for the next, I stopped on the platform and a great smile crossed my face. Travelers there probably thought, "Well she's finally lost it," because no one else looked happy. I was elated because I had some one-dollar bills in my purse. "So?" you may ask. Well, those dollar bills meant that I could buy a bag of cotton candy from the little guy that sells them on the platform and give a dollar to the guys who play the drums all evening long there. My dollar certainly would not change their lives, but for a moment when they smiled, it changed mine and my attitude! Boy was I happy!

Happiness seems to be at the heart of every

struggle. You know, people work hard at jobs so that they can make money to eat, buy a house, car, take a vacation... things that make them happy. People look for love so that they can be happy. Happiness is sometimes treated like a bad word... so some people say, I want love because I have so much of it to give away. If you believe that, then there's a bridge I would like to sell you. Really, it's OK to admit that we want it. Yes we do. We want to be happy. We want a promotion, a wedding, a divorce, children, a vacation, a day off, good health, a quarter pounder with cheese because that's what we think it will take to get us to that point of happiness.

I'm referring to the "now" feeling that would crinkle those eyes reading this, turn the sides of those lips upwards and make your face beam and heart smile.

Being happy is not a sin! God's word says it like this: John 16:33 "I have told you these things, so that in me you may have peace. In this world you will have trouble. But be of good cheer! I have overcome the world." "Be of good cheer" means "get happy". "Yaaaay!" Our God has already whipped the derrière of every problem that may come against you!

To be truly happy does not depend on anyone or anything. It's about you and your mind. Figure out when your mind is at peace, and get there again. AND, try this exercise... SMILE. Awww... come on... just try it. Bigger. I ate most of the cotton candy, and smiled the rest of the way home.

# WAITING FOR TOYS

 February 20th is my nephew Xavier's birthday. Since I live on the East Coast, I mailed his gift to him directly from Toys R US. His mom said he was wiggling like a worm with excitement waiting for the postman to arrive. Being the melodramatic young man that he is, she said he "whoooo hooooed" and danced around when he saw the present. All the while, my "little heart" Shuggie (that's my 2 year old niece) was watching her brother and wondering "where is my gift?" I can only imagine what she was thinking, "Aunty never sends him something without sending me something." Her mom said she asked, "Where is mine?" If you know me and what that baby means to me, you know I wanted to send her something too. It took every bit of self control I could muster to not add a little girlie gift to the order. But it was Xavier's day, not Shuggie's.

Sometimes when we see God blessing others, we are like Shugg. "God, I'm your kid too, where's mine?" I feel like I understand the heart of God a little better because He says, "I love you but today is your brother's turn." It's the Father's good pleasure to give us the kingdom." He said. When we position ourselves to receive, by believing in Him and obeying His word, He pours out His blessings so we don't have room to contain. Sometimes, like Shugg, we wait. But don't feel too bad for her or yourself, the waiting is NEVER more than you can bear! Her birthday is next week!

# MY OWN STIMULUS PACKAGE

It's all the talk around town, "the stimulus package." Who's getting it, who's not, will it make a difference or not? It's almost comical that from the mouths of investors and itinerants alike, everyone's wondering how much of the pie is theirs. Do you know what a stimulus package is? I mean on a really basic level? Webster says it's "something that rouses or incites to activity; incentive; stimulant; an agent that directly influences the activity of a living organism or one of its parts."

So a stimulus is something that "wakes up" a body that is asleep or inactive. It's really nothing new. It's always been a part of all our lives, we're constantly surrounded by things that affect us, make us react and influence us. EVERYDAY, all the time. In fact some of us have become so accustomed to it that we don't even recognize it and we need a whole STIMULUS PACKAGE just to wake us up in the morning. You know: 1 alarm, 4 snoozes and a blinding light... sometimes we have to throw in 4 stretches and 3 groans... then we move.

Today, recognize the things that you are allowing to affect you. In every situation you can make a conscious choice to react in a positive or negative way. That unreasonable co-worker, irate customer, noisy teenager, really late train, cab driver that flips you the bird (Can you tell I live in NYC?) all of those things are stimuli. How it affects you is up to you. Don't allow one bad word to spoil your entire day.

Before you do anything ask God to "Preserve your heart and your mind." That's the secret to keeping the bad stimuli out: God says, "He will keep him or her in PERFECT PEACE whose mind is on HIM." Think about His love and goodness today and let that be your stimulus. I tell you what... it's the ONLY no fail, guaranteed, destined to win every time way to have a fantastic day.

# I HAVE THE SCARS TO PROVE IT

Yesterday I did one of my least favorite things... ever, I visited the doctor. It was my annual visit but this was my first in New York City. A new doctor, so I had to go through my entire medical history and the whole experience to me is a harrowing one. Something struck me though... the lady kept looking at me with doubt as I spoke to her. I told her that I had surgery at 21 years old, then again 4 years later and about the miracle that God did in my body.

Anyone who has not come face to face with a miracle working God would understandably be confused, I guess. I know she was wondering, "why if you had these surgeries do you not have the side-effects... you must be a druggie or something" "That's why it's called a miracle, lady," I wanted to say but it was late and I was mellow.

Half way into the visit though, she believed. No, It wasn't my power of persuasion, my winning personality or a grammy worthy performance that convinced her that I was telling the truth... it was the scars. The scars were there to prove that my ovaries had once been removed, even though they were now there. Though faded, they are still obviously there, and she was quiet for a while.

Takes me right back in the bible to where Thomas couldn't believe that the man standing in front of Him was our risen Savior who was crucified. And Jesus said, "Put your finger here; see my hands. Reach out your hand and put it into my side. Stop doubting and believe." Thomas never had to touch Him, he just saw the scars. Those scars were the ones He received in His hands as they nailed Him to a tree, and as they pierced His side." Scars He bears as a reminder of what He did for you. He was pierced for our transgressions, He was crushed for our iniquities, the punishment that brought us peace was upon him, and by His wounds we are healed.

For those of you who must see the scars to believe, that's OK. We all have a little bit of doubting Thomas in us. But.. blessed are those who have not seen and yet believe. And the best part about that doctor's visit? It's OVER!

# I LOVE THE WEATHERMAN...

One night while he was still in med school, Curt drove around for more than 1 hour looking for a parking spot. He was so tired and frustrated by that time that he parked in an "alternate side" spot, right in front of a grade school. This meant that the next day, Monday morning, a day when he has exams first thing, he would have to wake up early and go move the car... and hope to find a spot and still make it on the train in time. The thought of driving around for another hour on a Monday morning, would be enough to even make a slug hyperventilate (and I bet that's not easy).

So last night he went to sleep with a heavy heart and the last thing he said was, "I wish they could suspend the parking rules tomorrow." This morning as I am brushing my teeth, he said, "It snowed", and he was smiling. If you've ever lived in New York and had to commute to work, you know those are not friendly words at all... and certainly not first thing on a freezing Monday morning! But snow means that "alternate side parking" is suspended! He doesn't have to move the car!

While adults all over the Tri-state area are probably grumbling, Curt and all the kids who have a "snow-day" are doing the "joy dance." God knows the desires of our hearts. You might say, GOD has nothing to do with the weather... and I'd politely correct you... He has everything to do with it. HE's the perfect weatherman. "The winds obey His voice and He sends the rain on the just and the unjust" and would He do this just for Curt? Absolutely! He'd give a nation for a son... what's a little white fluff? And today it just didn't snow... we have a storm! Now if only they could cancel work.

# HAPPY BIRTHDAY DADDY!!!

There are two adults I know that love their birthdays and look forward to it every single year... one is my dad and the other is me!

Today I remember the stories that my dad told me as I was growing up... my favorite were the ones from his childhood. Honestly, I cried over most of those stories, sometimes because they broke my heart hearing about the difficult times and at other times because they were so funny I laughed till I cried. They are still my favorite stories. I remember the ones about him not having shoes, his parents and siblings and his trips to the bay to get fish. They are as vivid in my mind as if I were there.

Today I would like him to know that I love and appreciate him. He defied many odds to become the man that he is today and he has taught me how to stand up for what I believe in, and most of all for WHOM I believe in. There is no greater lesson and no greater purpose in my life than my Faith in Christ Jesus and daddy is the one that introduced me to Him. See... I'm all teary eyed again.

This may not affect your life as it has mine... but that's exactly what's on my mind! Maybe we could celebrate my earthly dad's birthday like we celebrate my Heavenly Father's! That way I get gifts too!

# A DEDICATION TO 2 PEOPLE

As the arrows leave the bow of the skilled archer
The word of God never misses...never falters.
You stand and watch with bated breath
Anxious to see,
waiting to feel,
ready to dance
In the first and last rain.

God knows the very quiet prayers of your heart.
Even the ones you may not fully understand yourself,
He understands.
He has already been working on the things
That now arise as mountains before you...
Diligently
Faithfully,
And He's not the least bit worried that you will fail.

With each new morning sunrise, that stubborn shadow
Threatens to steal its warmth

But keep your eyes on the one who created the morning,
Who rides on the wings of the sunrise
Watching you
Keeping you
Working things all out for your good.

So rise up like the remnant you are!
Secure in His abundant love for you
And in His own words, "Fear not my child
You are mine
Engraved on the palm of my hand
I know you
I see you
And NO ONE can pluck you out of my hand."

# MY BEAUTIFUL MACHINE

You know how sometimes people say they woke up with a song in their heart? Uh-huh, well today I woke up with more of a low pitched moan. A bit like the lowest note on a trombone. It's one of those days when my mind wants to wake up but my body is in rebellion. I had a late night at church. It was amazing, but I'm tired.

So this is for those of you running on half a tank today. Picture a car... a nice dark grey Audi A8 and it's early morning. The car is gorgeous, like you and I, but it's dormant and it only has half a tank of gas. Then someone activates the starting device (most of these do not have "keys"). What do you think happens to that beautiful piece of engineering? Does it sputter and spit? Cough and wheeze? Groan and droop?

Nope. Instead it comes to life with a steady purr... and... just sits there. It will continue to just sit there... indefinitely... forever... until the gas runs out... until someone... steps on that accelerator. Then, and only then, can that machine reach it's full potential. When someone, who can drive, directs that car with a skillful hand.

This morning... I will allow the masterful Creator to lead and guide. Even when I'm on half a tank, He can bring me to my beautiful and fullest potential. He said that I am His masterpiece, fearfully and wonderfully made and so are you. He rejoices over us with singing. I can already feel my low groan waking up into a "ready-to-go" hum. May God be your pilot, the wind in your sails, whatever the problem, you never can fail. No foe can defeat you, 'cause you know within... With God as your pilot, you're destined to win!

# ON A MORE SERIOUS NOTE...

When people chide you or think you're "unenlightened and simple" because you are a believer, it's no small thing, NO. It's actually a privilege... a chance for you to determine what really is inside you, a chance to stand up and be identified with the Great King of Heaven. For some, it's not an easy thing.

A friend of mine choked back his own tears as he told me, "I want to become a Christian, but my father told me that if I do then I have to change my name because they would disown me." He's an adult that is torn by his love for his family and his encounter with the True and Living God.

More than 50 years ago, my Godmother, who was then 18 years old, left her home at gunpoint because someone found out that she became a follower of Christ. No one had "converted" her. She found a bible in a field and would steal away in the afternoons to read it. She discovered the truth with Holy Spirit as her teacher, a teenager alone who read that "God so loved the world that He gave His only Son."

But she discovered something that my friend has yet to figure out, "there is no person who has given up mother or father, houses or lands, or anything for HIS sake, who shall not be repaid, many times more, IN THIS LIFE". In Christ you DON'T lose!

Eventually, my Godmother became her family support, to the same brother that once held a gun to her she was a mother and friend. Whenever there was trouble, she was the one they would run to, because they knew she had a connection with the Living God who answers prayer!

So I am excited for my friend because the Big God of Heaven has stood up to intervene on His behalf and I am already in awe. Today, as you read, May your prayers be answered, your burdens be lifted, your faith be increased and your joy be full!

You are safe in the hands of your God, the great I AM.

# READ ON MONDAY

This evening when I get out of work, it will still be daylight! I'm excited about that. Sure, it will be the same time as usual... but it won't feel like it! Sure, I had one hour less to sleep on Sunday morning, but it's worth it to me, to not feel like I spent all my daylight hours behind a desk.

Since I overslept about an half an hour this morning, I just wanted to say a quick "Happy Monday." May yours fly swiftly by because it's filled with happy moments. You know what happens when you're having fun. You know the great thing about God is that He's the same... every day. I try to be, but some days just make me happier than others, mostly by not being Monday. But God is the God of Mondays and that includes this one.

So be renewed today, in your mind, your body and Spirit. For this day is one of those when no weapon formed against the child of God will prosper, in which He has given His angels charge over you, and you will run and not grow weary, walk and not faint because as you wait on Him, He renews your strength!

# THIS TASTES LIKE...

Would you rather be extremely busy or extremely bored? Be careful how you answer. I can almost see the myriad of your responses, fantastically parading through the center stage of my mind... but I am not yet certain where I stand on the matter. I know a little girl whose most prolific turn of phrase would be, "I am so bored." She's 9. If you're like me, you're thinking, "Those were the days, not a care in the world."

At 9 I was the center of attention at Freeport Presbyterian school, parading my math copy book through all the classrooms at the behest of a teacher that was smitten by its neatness and accuracy. At 9 I wore my pig tails tight and it didn't give me a headache. I put that liquid white polish on my shoes so much in the morning that when I took my socks off in the evening my feet looked like I stuck them in buckets of white paint.

One day I sat at the front of the class and at 9 years old I sweated drops the size of cannon balls as I tried to reproduce a drawing of my father for my teacher. I told him I had done the original. I had lied. He knew it. He never said, "you are lying" or "I don't believe you", He just said, "draw another one". That would have been the right time to fess up but strangely enough, at 9 years old my pride seemed worth saving. I learned a valuable lesson that day, scratching wretched lines into paper that I prayed would turn into the face of my father... "defending a lie is never worth the time, effort or energy." It's also quite embarrassing.

2 or 3 grueling hours after my first line, the teacher looked me in the eyes and said, "Are you done?" I stared ruefully at the pitiful caricature that gazed at me from the paper looking like a Picasso on crack and said, "Yes Sir, I'm finished." And that was it. Lesson learned. Sometimes the truth grates our insides on the way out. It's bitter in the mouth and may rob us of instant gratification, but it is that Truth you know that will always set you free. There may be no accolades attached or recognition afforded, but there will be freedom in your mind, with no strings attached. That why the bible records that "The power of life and death are in what we say. "

I spent the next few years of my life devouring portrait lessons from my father, from books and sketching everyone I knew. I actually became decent at it and even earned some money in High School doing portraits. One thing for sure though... I don't recall being bored. I was way too busy getting into and out of sticky situations to ever be bored, so maybe my little friend is just fine.

# 10 THINGS I SURELY KNOW

I just had a birthday… a month ago. So, in acknowledgement of traditions of reminiscence on such occasions… I decided to write down a few things I have learnt. These are nuggets of wisdom garnered over my years of planet wandering and observation. God knows there remains so much to discover, experience and even reject, but some truths are concrete to me…

1. Unless you're a synchronized swimmer, you're far less graceful in the water than you imagine.
2. The day I am convinced that I don't need to change is the day I become useless.
3. Uncomfortable shoes hurt less if you're having a great time.
4. It takes me months to lose 5 pounds and minutes to gain them back.
5. People mostly sing sweeter in their minds.

6. Spelling is a lost art and every generation practices it less.
7. People say talk is cheap... but what you say can cost you everything.
8. Fasting really is not fun. Needful, important... but not fun.
9. God sees. God hears. God knows.
10. Every moment can be an AMAZING one. EVERY single one can matter... even this one.

I still stagger at the place I am in life; compared to the place I was mere months ago. It seems I will never "settle down." Praise be to God that I don't see life pass by like airplanes while I sit lifeless and watch. Thank God that there are joys and sorrows, achievements and disappointments, wins and losses to make my journey FULL. Praise Jesus that in my victories I am carried on His ample shoulders and on the days that I dangle breathless over a precipice, I cling, inseparable from His mighty hand. Thank you, Jesus, for life!

# BERNIE MADOFF AND PURIM?

Yesterday my Jewish friends celebrated the feast of Purim. It's a funny sort of feast to me. While all the Jewish feasts are linked to the deliverance of the Jewish nation from bondage, this one is essentially deliverance from the sick and foolish pride of one man. Haman was highly upset to say the least, because Mordecai, and the Jews by proxy would not bow to him and pay him homage. In more modern vernacular he would be the celebrity who walked into Mordecai's restaurant and was dissed. He wasn't immediately ushered to a table, but had to stand in line like everyone else.

Well Mordecai didn't just write a scathing epistle to the New York Post, nor did he just hold a peaceful protest outside the Whitehouse, NO. He built a gallows to hang Mordecai on and had the King sign a decree that whoever didn't pay what he thought was proper homage to the King (By bowing to Haman) should be "destroyed."   I can almost hear the evil cartoon villain laughter in the background.

Then comes Esther, Mordecai's cousin, the Queen. What ensues is a battle of wits and cunning and the courage of a girl who was ready to give her life for her people. Esther's courage is noble, but honestly, Mordecai made it utterly clear to her that if she didn't stand up to fight for the Jews then God would find someone else to do it.

My favorite part of the Purim story remains this though: One insomniac night, the King was reading through the books and came across the record of Mordecai upsetting a plot to assassinate him. Upon inquiring he found that no one had thanked Mordecai for saving the king's life. No medal of bravery, no keys to the city... nothing.

So the next day the King calls Haman in and asks him what he should do to honor someone who deserves it. Here's the kicker: Haman thought the King wanted to honor him! So he devises what would be the equivalent of a motorcade and Macy's-esque parade broadcast on every television network, with the banners and announcers shouting, "This is how the King honors someone who deserves it." I'm sure Haman already saw himself waving ceremoniously at the adoring fans and wiping crocodile tears from his scheming eyes.

The King loved the idea and told Haman to see that all of that was done... to Mordecai!!! That's like someone all along investing Mr. Bernie Madoff's own millions in ice fishing in Ghana! To add insult to injury, Haman was the one appointed to lead Mordecai's horse shouting at the top of his lungs, "This is how the king honors someone who deserves it!" Can you imagine Haman's face as he paraded Mordecai through the streets?

Nobody likes an underdog story more than I but I think there's more than one great moral to this story. Here's One, "It must suck to have to walk through the streets shouting compliments to someone you despise" or some variation thereof. So today lets be sure not to think more highly of ourselves than we ought to and do unto others as we would have done to us. So now you know about Purim.

# HAVE YOU HEARD THIS ONE?

When I worked in Manhattan I promised a client a joke, by e-mail, because he was having a bad day. I must admit, it was a minor misrepresentation of my talents because anyone who has heard me speak knows that while I love humor and I love to laugh, so far, I basically stink at joke telling.

I remember standing before crowds and verging on erupting with laughter because the joke I was telling was so funny to me, and admittedly very few others. Often I must admit though, by the time I compose myself and wipe the tears from my eyes from laughing so much, people in the congregation are laughing too but rarely at the joke. People, even friends have said, that much funnier than my jokes, is the way I am the only one that thinks they're funny.

The bible advises that a merry heart is like medicine. It's true and it follows that a depressed heart is like poison. Laughter is contagious and pure laughter is the best kind. You know, like the laughter that comes out of a tickled baby. It's not the result of someone else's demise or loss but a spontaneous, uncontrived expression of amusement.

I think as we grow older, we forget what its like to just throw our heads back and laugh at things. You know what scientists say about laughing right? How it adds years to your life and improves your quality of life, then why is it such an act of congress for people to do it? I think the older we get we think it may make us look weak, or maybe simple. I don't know. We have enough youth. How about a fountain of "Smart"?

To me, the best company is the person who is not afraid to laugh at himself. I still believe, he who laughs last thinks slowest. You might say, "I have nothing to laugh about", and to that I humbly respond, "find something." Looking in the mirror can often trigger my laugh reflex, try it. If all else fails and as a last resort, I can always tell you one of my jokes. By the way, I haven't heard back from my client yet!

Proverbs 17:22 (NIV) A cheerful heart is good medicine, but a crushed spirit dries up the bones.

# A MESSAGE FROM THE AUTHOR

This book contains moments of my life that span two decades. It's sole purpose was to encourage you to smile. If you've been anyway affected or would like to share your thoughts about any entry with me... I'd love to hear from you.

You can always find me at www.PastorSharo.com or at www.HopeNYC.com.

At www.PastorSharo.com you will also find archives of messages, study materials and sign up for a free gift from Hope Press.

Follow me on twitter at #sharosharo

Facebook: www.facebook.com/sharoathope

And remember, if you're ever in New York, come visit me at:

Hope NYC church
142-82 Rockaway Blvd
Jamaica, NY 11436